THE
CURTIS-BENNETT
CHRONICLE

THE
CURTIS-BENNETT
CHRONICLE

Susan
Curtis-Bennett

The story of the legal family
and the genes which made them

Phillimore

1998

Published by
PHILLIMORE & CO. LTD.
Shopwyke Manor Barn, Chichester, West Sussex

ISBN 1 86077 082 7

Printed and bound in Great Britain by
BOOKCRAFT LTD.
Midsomer Norton, Avon

I dedicate this book to my third cousin, twice-removed, John Watkins, OBE. He introduced me to genealogy following the 1982 publication of his prize-winning book, *Dear Descendants* (privately published, Melbourne, ISBN 0 9592967 0 0) and encouraged me to research further into our mutual Bennett ancestry. A steady stream of letters from 1986 onwards has been a tremendous source of inspiration and led me eventually to widen my investigations into other branches of the family.

I would like to thank my cousin, Geoffrey Bennett, also third and twice-removed cousin, who took me to many places connected with the family, and whose pedigree charts are the basis of many printed in this volume. He read my manuscript and made many useful suggestions. Another cousin, Nancy Robinson Flannery, gave me much practical help and encouragement for which I am most grateful. I would like also to express my gratitude to the staff of various record offices and libraries around the country, and to a number of clergy who have so generously and patiently answered my enquiries.

Susan Curtis-Bennett

LIST OF ILLUSTRATIONS
AND PEDIGREES

Pedigree Charts

ACKNOWLEDGEMENTS

The author is grateful to the following people for permission to reproduce illustrations: Mrs. Margot Pollock, Mr. David Curtis-Bennett, Lady Drinkwater, Mrs. Serena Ballin, Mrs. Joan Shihwarg, Sir Henry Rumbold, Mrs. Virginia Gallico, Public Record Office, Controller of the Stationery Office, British Library, Registrar General of Scotland, Colchester Borough Council, Provost of Chelmsford Cathedral, Country Houses Association.

LIST OF SUBSCRIBERS

Serena M.A. Ballin
Susan J.M. Barnett (née Bennett)
Anne Beatrice Bennett
Elmira L.M.R.M. Bennett
Eric (F.W.) Bennett
G.L. Bennett
Country Houses Association
Deborah Cassidi
Mark Curtis-Bennett
Deirdre Drinkwater
Nancy Robinson Flannery
Caroline Fleming
Mrs. Paul Gallico
Patsy Giblin (née Dangar)
R.V. Hughes-Hallett
Margaret Lester (née Watkins)
Anne Neame (née Hughes Hallett)
Margaret Duncan Pollock
Peter Senn
Revd. William J.T. Smith
E.B.C. Thornton
Richard Thornton
Baroness Ludmila Verkade
John L. Watkins
Revd. A.C. Winter

PREFACE

To:
Mark Curtis-Bennett
Caroline Fleming (née Boscawen)
Diana Fielder (née Boscawen)
Victoria Payne (née Curtis-Bennett)
Lucy, James and George Fleming
Georgina and Edward Fielder
Charles and Alexander Payne

Dear Nephews and Nieces (or Nieces and Nephews),

It may be, in years to come, when you all are middle-aged and have children and grandchildren of your own, that you will begin to look back and be curious to know more about your ancestors. I trust that I am now in a position to satisfy that curiosity, having spent the last ten years or so on an extensive research programme. My Australian cousin, John Watkins, left a few unanswered questions about the origins of the Bennett family in his book, *Dear Descendants*. In 1986, he asked me to undertake further investigations. I am very glad that I did this, as I have found genealogy to be a most absorbing and fascinating hobby: history on an individual basis, you might say. As my hunt has progressed, I have had a wonderfully enjoyable time uncovering layers of history. It has also been a voyage of self-discovery.

I hope you will derive some satisfaction and entertainment from the result. My search has taken me from Exeter to Colchester, from Yorkshire to Wiltshire, from England to Scotland and Wales. Among our forebears you will find lawyers, doctors of medicine and divinity, Lords of the Manor and City merchants, Welsh princes, gourmets, go-getters and even an Elizabeth Taylor. Many of my discoveries have resulted from following the sometimes ignored female lines. Our family comes from all parts of Britain and perhaps also from France. Some have found prosperity in Australia and America. It has been a great joy to discover and get to know new relatives.

This research is far from complete. There remains, at the time of writing, the mystery of the origins of Joseph Bennett, from whom we derive our surname. Perhaps more data will come to light as further records are released. Maybe one of you will feel inspired to continue the search. So now I come to the end of my quest. I've had the excitement of the chase, but a considerable effort has been involved. I've risen at dawn to spend a day on the Welsh borders, heaved heavy tomes in many a library and record office, to come away with – if I've been lucky – perhaps one new name, fact or date. But it has been a labour of love. I hope that you, my collateral descendants, will think it has been worthwhile.

Susan Curtis-Bennett

October 1998

Explanatory note: the superscript numbers which appear in the text apply to the reference notes at the end of each Part. The numbers (1)–(11) before people's names in the pedigree charts refer to key individuals whose ancestry can thus be traced in further charts. These people are: Mary Butterfield (1), George Peter Bennett (2), Augustus Frederick Bennett (3), Emily Hughes-Hallett (4), Elsie Dangar (5), Margaret Mackintosh (6), Mary Hallett (7), Frances Knatchbull (8), Mary Crowley (9) Sara Baskerville (10) and Sir James Baskerville (11). I have also capitalised the names of other personalities in these charts, for easy identification.

For reasons of space, I have been unable to include additional spouses where no offspring have resulted. I have also been unable to include every family member of every branch (for instance, the Dangar family), and therefore have restricted myself to those mentioned in the text. But I hope that all future generations will be able to trace their own particular ancestry with the knowledge that they already have of their parents and grandparents. It has been impossible to record all first names on the charts, also for reasons of space, but I hope to have made up for this in the index.

PART 1

WHERE DO WE ORIGINATE?
THE BENNETT HERITAGE

Samuel Bennett, BD, christened in St Margaret's, Westminster; The Wiltshire Bennetts and Benetts; 'Mad Jack Benett'; did sailor Sam marry in Gibraltar?; 'Pompous Percy' Bennett; The Witham Bennetts – a drysalter in the City; George II and the fatal cricket ball; desperately seeking Joseph – killed by cricket or tennis ball?

Pythouse, Wiltshire – the ancestral home?

There is absolutely no problem in tracing our ancestry on the Bennett side back to Samuel Bennett, Bachelor of Divinity (BD) who was baptised at St Margaret's, Westminster, official church of the House of Commons, on 1 November 1741. I found Samuel's baptismal certificate, together with his ordination papers, in the Guildhall Library, London.[1] These show that he was born on 1 October 1741. He was succeeded by his son, another Samuel, this time a Doctor of Divinity (I shall frequently refer to these two just as BD and DD, as they are known in the family). DD's son, George

1   Samuel Bennett, BD's baptismal certificate (Guildhall Library MS 10326/98).

Peter, also entered the church. Then followed three lawyers: Sir Henry, the first Curtis Bennett [*sic*], Chief Metropolitan Magistrate; my grandfather, also Sir Henry; and my father, Frederick Henry, known as Derek (see Charts 1 and 2).

In case you do not know why the first Sir Henry became Curtis Bennett, here is the explanation: there were two Henry Bennetts at the Bar at that time, and solicitors used to get confused. So my great-grandfather, whose mother was a Charlotte Curtis, added his middle name to Bennett. He does not appear to have used the hyphen, as it does not appear on his tombstone, although his wife, Emily (who had a double-barrelled maiden name) does sign her married name with the hyphen.

What of BD's parentage? The baptismal certificate names his parents as Joseph and Jane. Here lies the mystery. This Joseph (like Samuel, a 17th-century Puritan name) has proved extremely elusive. Our family has long believed that we sprang from the Bennetts of Pythouse, Tisbury, Wiltshire, a well-established county family. My grandfather used to say: 'Pythouse is the cradle of the Bennetts'. George Peter, who I deduce wrote the entry in the family bible, claims as much. I do have some doubts about this entry as some of it seems to have been copied directly from J. Burke's *General Armory of England, Scotland and Ireland*.[2] There is at least one inaccuracy in the bible entry: William Coles Bennett, vicar of Corsham, was not a direct ancestor, as implied. Although descended from the Bennetts of Pythouse, he died in 1849, so he could not possibly be a forebear of Samuel BD.

2   Bennett family bible entry claims Joseph 'accidentally killed by cricket ball thrown by George the Second'.

The name of the Pythouse family is originally said to have been Pytt, derived from the French 'puits' for well. After the land on which the house stands was given to the family in 1225 by the Abbess of Shaftesbury, the name became Pytt-alias-Bennett, then eventually just Bennett. This was a tribute, no doubt, to the fact that Shaftesbury was a Benedictine foundation. The most noteworthy family member was Colonel Thomas Bennett, military secretary to Prince Rupert, nephew of Charles I and commander of the Royalist cavalry (see Chart 3). Colonel Bennett was present at the siege of Winchester, later commanded the Royalist forces who were defending Romsey against the Cromwellians, and played a prominent part in the defence of Plymouth. The Prince left Colonel

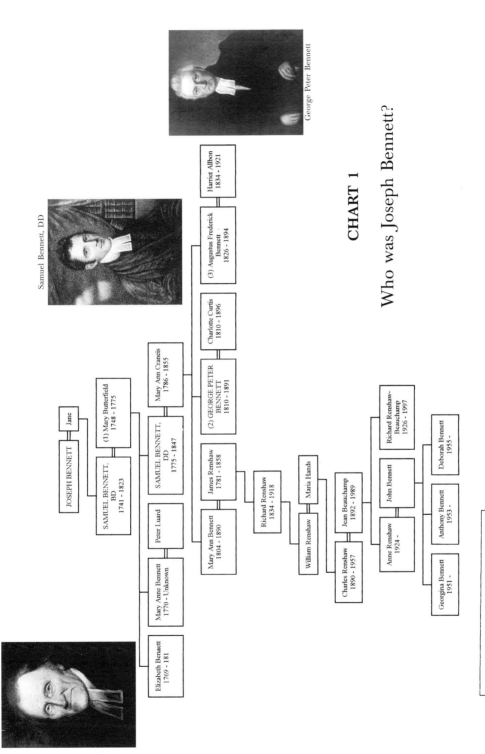

Samuel Bennett, BD

Samuel Bennett, DD

George Peter Bennett

CHART 1

Who was Joseph Bennett?

JOSEPH BENNETT — Jane

SAMUEL BENNETT, BD 1741 - 1823 — (1) Mary Butterfield 1748 - 1775

Elizabeth Bennett 1769 - 181

Mary Anne Bennett 1770 - Unknown — Peter Luard

SAMUEL BENNETT, DD 1775 - 1847 — Mary Ann Craneis 1786 - 1855

Mary Ann Bennett 1804 - 1890 — James Renshaw 1781 - 1858

(2) GEORGE PETER BENNETT 1810 - 1891 — Charlotte Curtis 1810 - 1896

(3) Augustus Frederick Bennett 1826 - 1894 — Harriet Allbon 1834 - 1921

Richard Renshaw 1834 - 1918 — Maria Hands

William Renshaw

Charles Renshaw 1890 - 1957 — Jean Beauchamp 1892 - 1989

Anne Renshaw 1924 - — John Bennett

Richard Renshaw-Beauchamp 1926 - 1997

Georgina Bennett 1951 -

Anthony Bennett 1953 -

Deborah Bennett 1955 -

Sources: family bible and pedigrees, Guildhall Library MS
10326~8; baptism register, Westminster Abbey library;
memorial tablets, Hatfield Peverel and Ulting churches,
Essex; "The Life of a Christian Minister", A.F Bennett, 1890

CHART 2
From Bennett to Curtis-Bennett

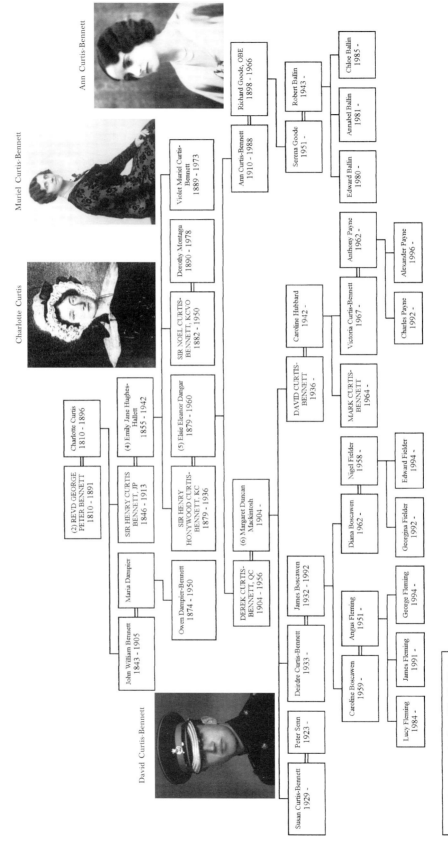

Ann Curtis-Bennett

Muriel Curtis-Bennett

Charlotte Curtis

David Curtis Bennett

Charlotte Curtis
1810 - 1896

(2) REVD GEORGE
PETER BENNETT
1810 - 1891

John William Bennett
1843 - 1905

Maria Dampier

Owen Dampier-Bennett
1874 - 1950

SIR HENRY CURTIS
BENNETT, JP
1846 - 1913

(4) Emily Jane Hughes-
Hallett
1855 - 1942

DEREK CURTIS-
BENNETT, QC
1904 - 1956

SIR HENRY
HONYWOOD CURTIS-
BENNETT, KC
1879 - 1936

(5) Elsie Eleanor Dangar
1879 - 1960

(6) Margaret Duncan
Mackintosh
1904 -

SIR NOEL CURTIS-
BENNETT, KCVO
1882 - 1950

Dorothy Montagu
1890 - 1978

Violet Muriel Curtis-
Bennett
1889 - 1973

Ann Curtis-Bennett
1910 - 1988

Richard Goode, OBE
1898 - 1966

Susan Curtis-Bennett
1929 -

Peter Senn
1923 -

Deirdre Curtis-Bennett
1933 -

James Boscawen
1932 - 1992

DAVID CURTIS-
BENNETT
1936 -

Caroline Hubbard
1942 -

Serena Goode
1951 -

Robert Ballin
1943 -

Caroline Boscawen
1959 -

Angus Fleming
1951 -

Diana Boscawen
1962 -

Nigel Fielder
1958 -

MARK CURTIS-
BENNETT
1964 -

Victoria Curtis-Bennett
1967 -

Anthony Payne
1962 -

Edward Ballin
1980 -

Annabel Ballin
1981 -

Chloe Ballin
1985 -

Lucy Fleming
1984 -

James Fleming
1991 -

George Fleming
1994 -

Georgina Fielder
1992 -

Edward Fielder
1994 -

Charles Payne
1992 -

Alexander Payne
1996 -

Sources: family papers and pedigrees; "Who Was Who"
1897-1916, 1929-40, 1951-60; newspaper obituary notices;
tombstones, Kelvedon churchyard, Essex; "Curtis", Derek
Curtis-Bennett and Roland Wild, Cassell, 1937

Bennett £800 in his will. After the Restoration, Thomas was elected MP for Shaftesbury. A portrait of him, holding a little King Charles spaniel, is attributed to Lely, and hangs in the Pythouse morning room. According to the Pythouse pedigree, he was buried at Holy Trinity, Shaftesbury where there was a monumental inscription to him. This has now disappeared as the church was closed in the early 1970s and put to other uses. I cannot find his tombstone either.

The Benetts of Pythouse and Norton Bavant

After the Civil War the Bennett family lost Pythouse largely because they were fined £1,000 for aiding the Royalists. Moreover, the Bennetts' resources were exhausted because of the effects of the Civil War on agriculture. The house was sold for £45,000 to a Peter Dove, Mayor of Salisbury, who lived there for 56 years. The Bennetts retreated to nearby Semley. In 1686 Colonel Bennett's sister, Patienta, married William Benett, Recorder of Shaftesbury, from the neighbouring but unrelated family at Norton Bavant, seven miles away. Their son, Thomas Benett, bought Pythouse back in 1725 for the surprisingly small sum of £7,300. But he was buying only the shell of the Elizabethan house, plus a small acreage around it. Although the Benetts had their own manor house at Norton Bavant – described by William Cobbett in his *Rural Rides* as 'one of the prettiest spots that my eyes have beheld' – they preferred the potential of the Pythouse site.

This lies in a splendid situation, with a magnificent view of hills, wood and valley, and is sheltered from the north by an abrupt hill covered with trees and shrubs. Thomas pulled down the Elizabethan structure and built the present Queen Anne/early Georgian house from Tisbury stone, forming the core of today's house. Later Benetts decorated the frontage with Palladian additions, doubling its size and

3   Pythouse, Tisbury, Wiltshire as rebuilt in 1805. An earlier, Elizabethan house was pulled down. (Photo courtesy of Country Houses Association.)

CHART 3
The Bennetts of Pythouse, Tisbury, Wiltshire

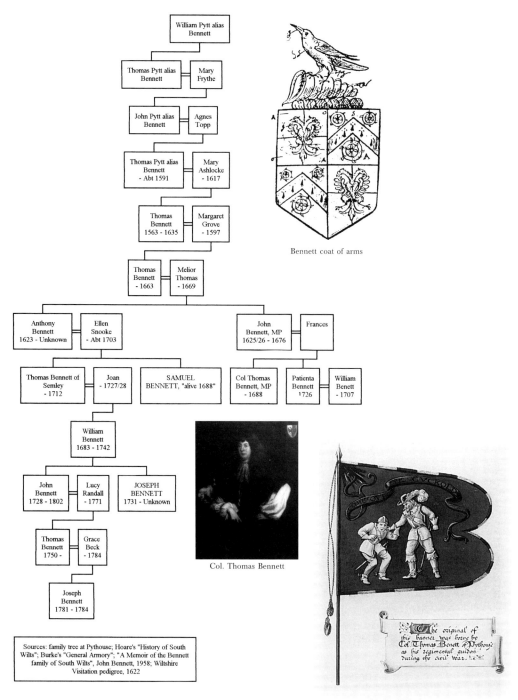

William Pytt alias Bennett

Thomas Pytt alias Bennett — Mary Frythe

John Pytt alias Bennett — Agnes Topp

Thomas Pytt alias Bennett - Abt 1591 — Mary Ashlocke - 1617

Thomas Bennett 1563 - 1635 — Margaret Grove - 1597

Thomas Bennett - 1663 — Melior Thomas - 1669

Anthony Bennett 1623 - Unknown — Ellen Snooke - Abt 1703

John Bennett, MP 1625/26 - 1676 — Frances

Thomas Bennett of Semley - 1712 — Joan - 1727/28

SAMUEL BENNETT, "alive 1688"

Col Thomas Bennett, MP - 1688

Patienta Bennett 1726

William Benett - 1707

William Bennett 1683 - 1742

John Bennett 1728 - 1802 — Lucy Randall - 1771

JOSEPH BENNETT 1731 - Unknown

Thomas Bennett 1750 - — Grace Beck - 1784

Joseph Bennett 1781 - 1784

Bennett coat of arms

Col. Thomas Bennett

his Civil War banner

The original of this banner was borne by Col Thomas Benett of Pythous as his regimental guidon during the civil war, &c.

Sources: family tree at Pythouse; Hoare's "History of South Wilts"; Burke's "General Armory"; "A Memoir of the Bennett family of South Wilts", John Bennett, 1958; Wiltshire Visitation pedigree, 1622

accommodation. A chapel was added, copied from part of Canterbury Cathedral, with a family vault underneath. But the Bishop of Salisbury refused to consecrate it because it was intended exclusively for private worship.

Thomas's granddaughter, Etheldred, was a notable collector of local fossils. This lady studied geology in its early days, and supplied R.C. Hoare with a catalogue of Wiltshire fossils for his county history. She sent a set of fossils to the museum in St Petersburg and was rewarded by the Tsar with an Honorary Doctorate of Civil Law in the University of St Petersburg. He thought by her name that she must be a man. Her niece Etheldreda founded the Sisters of Bethany, an Anglo-Catholic religious order. An appreciation of her[3] says that she was 'a woman of very great beauty and charm'. The article claims that among her family's collateral ancestors was Hereward the Wake, the English leader of a revolt against the Normans in 1070. This must be through Etheldreda's great-great-grandfather, William Wake.

Connections with the CABAL?

Paul Curtis-Bennett, a barrister cousin of my father, once suggested to me that I should try to find the family connection, if any, with Henry Bennett, Earl of Arlington, member of Charles II's CABAL (his inner cabinet) and his Lord Chamberlain. Arlington was educated at Westminster School and at Christ Church, Oxford, where his portrait by Lely hangs in the hall. The scar shown on his nose was the result of a wound he received in a skirmish at Andover where, naturally, he was a supporter of the Royalist cause. Suspected of being a secret Catholic, he was fluent in foreign languages, notably French, Spanish and Latin. He also bore the title of Viscount Thetford. Both Arlington Street and Bennet [sic] Street, off Piccadilly in London, are named after him. Through the marriage of his daughter, Isabella, to the Duke of Grafton, he is an ancestor of Diana, Princess of Wales.

Elizabeth Dowman, then assistant to the York Herald at the College of Arms, confirmed in her letter to me of 17 December 1986 that the arms of the Earl are remarkably similar to those of Benett of Norton Bavant. I have also seen claims in family papers of a definite relationship between Arlington and his elder brother Lord Ossulston and the Norton Bavant family. This is supported by Walford in his *County Families of the United Kingdom*[4] which claims that the Bennet [sic] ancestors of the Earl of Arlington and also the Earl of Tankerville were originally seated at Norton Bavant until the 15th century, when they moved to Essex. Incidentally, I notice in the Pythouse pedigree that Thomas Benett, father of the William who married Patienta Bennett, was a Captain in the Parliamentary Army. This is the only instance I can find in the whole of this family history of an ancestor who did not support the reigning monarch of the time.

'Mad Jack' Benett

The last Benett owner of Pythouse was Colonel John (Jack) Benett, a descendant of both families (see Chart 4). An old Etonian, he was a colourful character known locally as 'Mad Jack'. He put up notices saying 'Trespassers will be shot' and drove a large, open Rolls-Royce around the countryside, wearing a horsewhip round his neck. He owned a yacht and used to hunt big game in Africa and India. He fought in the Boer War and was also a war correspondent and a photographer in the Sudan. He claimed to have charged with the 21st Lancers at Omdurman, armed only with his camera and tripod and in the company of Winston Churchill. Jack was writing a history of the Benett family, but it was destroyed by his mother in a jealous rage. She was Ellen Stanford of Brighton, whose father died when she was three, leaving her a large fortune. Preston Manor, where the Stanfords lived, contains some memorabilia of Jack and his son Vere. My cousin Virginia Curtis-Bennett met Jack at Pythouse and was given a copy of *The Pythouse Papers* which are concerned with the wartime activities of local supporters of Charles I. These were found buried in a large chest when foundations were being dug for extensions to Pythouse in 1805.

The chest was not the only object found in Pythouse. In the cellars there is a mysterious coffin containing the skeleton of one Mary, or Molly, Peart, the last woman to be publicly hanged in this country in Oxford in about 1824. She had been a nursery maid at Pythouse and had borne a child which she killed. The identity of the father was never known though the butler was suspected. She was at first buried in a field in unhallowed ground, but John Benett, the then owner of Pythouse, was allowed to have the body exhumed. The body was articulated and the coffin was placed in the Pythouse cellar, where it remained for about a century. In 1933, Jack Benett thought that her body should be a museum piece, so the coffin was taken to Brighton to be put on display. Strange noises in the night followed at Pythouse and misfortunes befell the Benett family. Mary Peart was known to have threatened to haunt the house if she was ever moved from there. So the coffin, with its small glass front, was brought back to the house and remains there to this day.

Jack Benett died in 1947 and his wife, Evelyn, ten years later. Both their children, Vere and Patience, died young, Vere of wounds suffered in World War One (WW1), where he served as a Captain in the Royal Artillery. Pythouse was left by Jack's widow to a distant cousin, Sir Anthony Rumbold, grandson of the Ambassador under whom Percy Bennett, a diplomat member of the family, served in Vienna. Today Pythouse is a condominium run by the Country Houses Association and accommodates a number of tenants.

Both Jack and Evelyn and their children are buried in the 12th-century All Saints' church at Norton Bavant. There are plaques and brass effigies to the memory of various members of the Benett family in a chapel dedicated to them. Particularly impressive is a monumental brass to a Joh'es (or John) Benet and his wife. He was an important cloth manufacturer who died in 1461 and the implements of his trade are shown. Miss P. Shields, the genealogist who donated the pedigree covering both Bennetts and Benetts which hangs in the first-floor long gallery at Pythouse, gives as one of her sources *The Life and Times of Ralph Allen* by R.E.M Peach.[5] This book gives a detailed Norton Bavant Benett pedigree, stretching back to Robert Benet, Keeper of the King's Seal in England in 1189, and a John Benet of Wiltshire who was appointed Governor of Monmouth Castle by the King in 1327.

CHART 4

The Benetts of Norton Bavant and Pythouse, Wiltshire

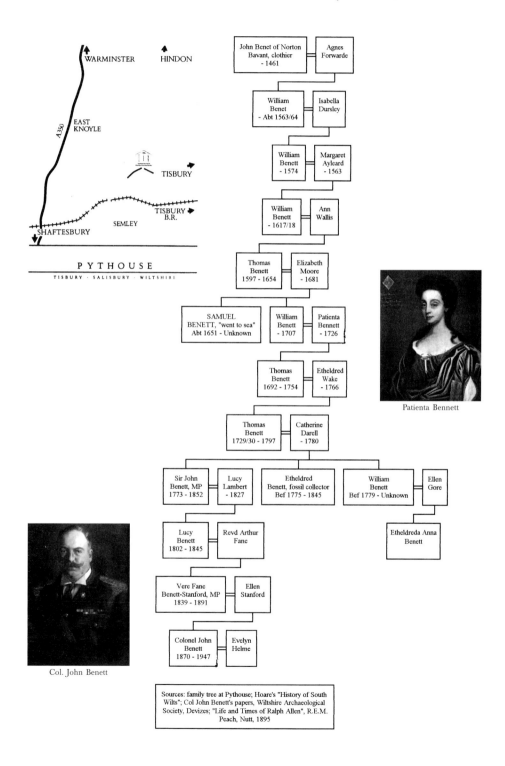

WARMINSTER · HINDON

A350

EAST KNOYLE

TISBURY

TISBURY B.R.

SEMLEY

SHAFTESBURY

P Y T H O U S E

TISBURY · SALISBURY · WILTSHIRE

John Benet of Norton Bavant, clothier - 1461	Agnes Forwarde
William Benet - Abt 1563/64	Isabella Dursley
William Benett - 1574	Margaret Ayleard - 1563
William Benett - 1617/18	Ann Wallis
Thomas Benett 1597 - 1654	Elizabeth Moore - 1681

SAMUEL BENETT, "went to sea" Abt 1651 - Unknown	William Benett - 1707	Patienta Bennett - 1726

Thomas Benett 1692 - 1754	Etheldred Wake - 1766

Patienta Bennett

Thomas Benett 1729/30 - 1797	Catherine Darell - 1780

Sir John Benett, MP 1773 - 1852	Lucy Lambert - 1827	Etheldred Benett, fossil collector Bef 1775 - 1845	William Benett Bef 1779 - Unknown	Ellen Gore

Lucy Benett 1802 - 1845	Revd Arthur Fane

Etheldreda Anna Benett

Vere Fane Benett-Stanford, MP 1839 - 1891	Ellen Stanford

Col. John Benett

Colonel John Benett 1870 - 1947	Evelyn Helme

Sources: family tree at Pythouse; Hoare's "History of South
Wilts"; Col John Benett's papers, Wiltshire Archaeological
Society, Devizes; "Life and Times of Ralph Allen", R.E.M.
Peach, Nutt, 1895

Several Samuels and Josephs – possible ancestors?

So where does our Bennett family come into the picture? There are Josephs and Samuels in the Pythouse first-floor pedigree who offer possibilities, taking into account the naming patterns popular at the time. For instance, a possible predecessor could be the Samuel Bennett, said on the pedigree at Pythouse to be 'alive in 1688' (see Chart 3) when he was mentioned in his father's will. His parents, Anthony Bennett and Ellen Snooke, were married in 1641 and he, the second child, was followed by five other children. So his birthdate, I estimate, would be in the late 1640s or early 1650s. Samuel, as second son, would have had every reason to leave Wiltshire and seek his fortune elsewhere. But I have no details of his life and there is no proof that we ascend to him. The trouble with this theory, to my mind, is that there is a considerable generation gap between this Samuel and our Joseph and Samuel – especially at a time when life expectancy was nothing like it is today. I am afraid that we are caught here in what is known as the Commonwealth Gap. During the period 1649-60 very few church and therefore baptismal records were kept and many existing ones were destroyed. That is probably why I have been unable to trace Samuel's birthdate. I suppose it is possible that Samuel was the *grandfather* of our Joseph.

Other family papers claim ascent to another Samuel on the Pythouse chart who also appears in R.C. Hoare's *Modern History of South Wiltshire*[6] as a member of the Norton Bavant Benetts, and as having 'gone to sea' (see Chart 4). Samuel, the son of Thomas Benett and his second wife, Elizabeth Moore (whom he married in 1627), was baptised at Norton Bavant on 7 May 1651 and mentioned in his father's will in 1654. He is a possible candidate for the fatherhood of Joseph. But again there would have been a gap of 90 years between him and his grandson Samuel BD. I have searched several times, without success, for further evidence of Samuel's naval career in the appropriate archives at the Public Record Office (PRO) at Kew. He just does not appear in the list of commissioned officers for the period. Nor does his brother, Richard, who, according to some family papers, also went to sea.

'A Cargo of oyle and fruite'

Their maternal grandfather, Thomas Moore of Bristol, was a Merchant Venturer with shipping interests. In 1660, he sailed as a 'factor' aboard the *Endeavour* to Ireland and from there to Leghorn in the Mediterranean, arriving back in Bristol with a cargo of '190 peeces of oyle and 150 barrels of fruite'.[7] Thomas, the son of Edward Moore, also a merchant, was one of the Society of Merchant Venturers' two Wardens from 1662-63 and again from 1664-65. The Society was constituted in a charter granted by Charles I and over the next three centuries the names of many of Bristol's leading citizens appeared on its roll of members. In an age when exploration was taking hold of the nation's imagination, its members played a leading part in the discovery of new lands. It is possible that Thomas might have given a job to his grandson, Samuel, already 24 when Thomas died in 1675.

However, Samuel is definitely described in family papers as belonging to the Royal Navy, not the Merchant, although at that time men did transfer from one service to another. The only clue I have at all about this Samuel's career occurs in a letter among Jack Benett's papers in the Wiltshire Archaeological Society's archives in Devizes. This letter, written on 15 July 1907 by Dick Dampier-Bennett, a grandson of George Peter Bennett, from Bennett & Co, merchants of 16 Victoria Street, London SW, contains the following sentences:

> I think my father's supposition … is probably correct, viz that the Joseph Bennett who was killed by George II was the son of the Samuel Bennett who went to sea and was married at Gibraltar. I forget the name of the lady. Can you find in your MSS or papers any mention of a Samuel Bennett who was a sailor?

Unfortunately I have found no reply to Dick's enquiry. Perhaps the information disappeared with the papers which Ellen Stanford, Jack Benett's mother, destroyed in a fit of peevishness. The British captured Gibraltar from the Spanish in 1704 – a bit late in Samuel's naval career for him to have taken part in the siege. However, I suppose it is possible that he visited the Rock on some previous occasion, found a bride there, and returned to England. Another possibility is that he settled down in London after a lifetime at sea and found a bride in that city. Elizabeth Moore's will, proved in 1682, mentions other sons and daughters and even grandchildren, but there is no mention of Samuel. Perhaps he had lost touch with the family by that time.

'Pompous Percy' Bennett

A pedigree prepared by Percy Bennett, CMG, my great-grandfather's diplomat cousin, also claims ascent to the Pythouse Bennetts – from Joseph, the son of William Bennett (see Chart 3). But this Joseph is shown quite clearly on the Pythouse pedigree as having been baptised on 13 April 1731. So it seems extremely unlikely that he could have fathered Samuel ten years later, unless his baptism was deferred for some reason, which did sometimes happen.

Percy, who served as HM Consul in New York, as Commercial Attaché in Vienna and lastly as Envoy Extraordinary and Minister Plenipotentiary in Venezuela, was a colourful character. He was a social success, playing golf with King Edward VII in Marienbad and receiving a wedding present from the Prince of Wales (later Duke of Windsor). He wrote his memoirs, *Reminiscences Connected with my Official Career, 1893-1927*,[8] and in them opines that his solution to most diplomatic problems was to 'give a series of big dinner parties'. In Vienna he served under Sir Horace Rumbold and recalls how, when arriving in the city, he was advised by the ambassador never to take his wife to the stalls at the opera – a box was *de rigueur*. Percy was nicknamed 'Pompous Percy' by his beautiful wife, Winifred Youell, in love letters she exchanged with Field Marshal Sir John French while he was commanding the British Expeditionary Force in France 1914-15. These letters came to light when Joan Shihwarg, her granddaughter, auctioned them at Sotheby's in 1975. The Imperial War Museum bought them for £4,800.

It was not Henry Carr (as in Sir Tom Stoppard's play *Travesties*) who was HM Consul General in Zurich in 1917, but Percy, as is acknowledged at the end of the play in which he is relegated to butler status. Henry Carr was in fact quite a junior member of the Consulate. Sir Tom referred me to Richard Ellman's book *James Joyce*[9] in which there are quite a few references to Percy: it seems that he was annoyed with Joyce, who was living in Zurich, for not reporting to him officially to offer his services in wartime, and treated him in an 'offhand and superior way' when Joyce called on him to get official support for a troupe of players he was forming. To get his own back Joyce composed rather an unkind limerick about Percy which ran:

> There's an anthropoid consul called Bennett
> With the jowl of a jackass or jennet
> He must muzzle or mask it
> In the waste paper basket
> When he rises to bray in the Senate.

Joyce also satirised Percy and Sir Horace Rumbold, then Minister in Berne and son of the Ambassador to Austria mentioned earlier, in *Ulysses*. Poor Percy, did he really deserve all this? He doesn't mention Joyce in his memoirs but says that the year and a half he spent in Zurich was interesting and exciting. 'Being so near the German border and in neutral country was paradise for spies, and the large staff and numerous motor cars at my disposal were kept fully occupied,' he wrote.

The Bennetts of Witham, Essex

Family papers suggest another possible Joseph Bennett as an ancestor. He is mentioned on page 34 of John Watkins' book, *Dear Descendants*. John based most of his information on the Bennetts on papers belonging to Paul Curtis-Bennett, presumably inherited from his father, Noel, or even his grandfather, the first Sir Henry Curtis Bennett. Samuel Bennett, BD, although born in London, spent all his adult life in Essex. The third son of Sir John Bennett of Witham, Essex, Judge of the Marshalsea Court (the debtors' court, as portrayed by Dickens in *Little Dorrit*) was a Joseph Bennett. He was born in 1685, after two brothers called John and Thomas, both of whom became barristers (see Chart 5).

Joseph, presumably named after his uncle, Sir Joseph Brand of Edwardstone, Suffolk, became a drysalter in the City of London. He would have dealt in dry or salted meats, pickles and sauces. Some family papers claim that he lived in Great George Street, Westminster, but I can find no confirmation of this from rate books of the period. Joseph, according to the diary[10] of his brother, Alexander, proved to be a bad businessman, and got into debt in 1734. However, Alexander, who had made a fortune in the East Indies, appears generously to have bailed out his brother. Alexander writes most touchingly in his diary as follows:

> Considering brother Joseph was born as good as myself, though now come to misfortunes and forsd to flye into Wales, wherefore resolved to compound his debts and bring him home again, which I succeeded in, and brought him and his wife unto London again, at above £300 charge, and trust in God shall not be the poorer for it, or my children after me.

CHART 5
The Bennetts of Witham, Essex

John Bennet, of Westminster, Esq. descended from the Bennets of Wiltshire : [of which family was Henry Bennet, late Earl of Arlington, and John Bennet Lord Ossulston]. He died in 1670, and left these lordships to his eldest son and heir—*John Bennet,* afterwards of Gray's-Inn, Esq. In 1699, he was made Judge of the Marshalsea Court; in 1705, created Serjeant at Law; and knighted 7th July 1706. He died 21st December 1723; having had issue, by Anne his wife, sister of the late Sir Joseph Brand, of Edwardston in Suffolk, Kt. four sons and one daughter; viz. John, a Barrister at Law, and one of the Masters in Chancery; 2. Thomas, also a Barrister at Law, and constituted Master in Chancery 10th June 1723; 3. Joseph, a drysalter in London; 4. Alexander, a merchant, who lived nine years in the East-Indies, and brought thence a considerable fortune. The daughter, named Anne, was married to the Honourable John Vaughan, Esq. eldest son of John Lord Viscount-Lisburne, in Ireland, by Mallet, one of the daughters and coheirs of John, late Earl of Rochester. Upon Sir John Bennet's death, his eldest son and heir —*John,* above-mentioned, succeeded to this estate.

[G] Bennet's Arms. Gules, a bezant, between three demi-lions rampant, argent.

Pedigree of Bennett,

enlarged from that in Le Neve's *Knights* and in Morant's *Essex* (such parts being here printed in *italics*) and other sources; the information taken from the *Diary of Alexander Bennett* (see *ante* pp. 145—154) being placed within inverted commas.

John Bennet, of Thames street, London, and St. Paul's, Covent Garden, Westminster, Esq., *purchased in 1668, of Capt.* ⊤ Sarah, executrix Jeremy Blackman, *the manor of Witham Magna, otherwise Neweland, in Witham, co. Essex; died 1670.* Will dat. 7 Aug. 1670 (directing his burial to be at Hertingfordbury, if he dies there), proved 25 Nov. 1670 in C.P.C. (157 Penn). | to her husband 25 Nov. 1670.

	(2)	(1)		
Sir John Bennet, of Witham afsd. *and afterwards of* ⊤ Anne, sister of Sir Joseph ⊤ Thomas Dudson,	*Sedgewick Park, in parish of Nuthurst, Sussex, under* age Aug. 1670; adm. to Gray's Inn, 2 Feb. 1674/5; *Serjeant-at-Law* (1705); *Steward of the Marshalsea of Her Majesty's Household and Judge of her Palace Court, 1699 to 1723; Knighted at Windsor Castle, on the delivery of the address from the County of Middlesex, 7 or 10 July 1706;* mar. (sett. 29 Nov. 1682) 9 Jan. 1682/3, at St. Dunstan's in the East, London, being then styled of Gray's Inn, Esq.; *died Sat. 21 and was bur. Monday 30 Dec. 1723 at Witham, co. Essex.* Will dat. 29 Nov. 1723, pr. 22 Jan. 1723/4, in C.P.C. (2 Bolton).	*Brand, of Edwardstone, co. Suffolk,* as also of Susan, wife of Sir John Morden, Baronet, (the founder of Morden College, Blackheath), being 6th and youngest da. of Joseph Brand or Brond, of Edwardstone afsd. (living 1664) by Thomazine, da. and coheir of Thomas Trotter, of London, merchant; she "died 5 Jan. 1721/2" and was bur. 15 at Witham.	of St. Benet's, Gracechurch, London, woollen draper; bap. there 9 Jan. 1648/9; mar. lic. (Fac. Office) 13 May 1676; bur. 21 Aug. 1678, at St. Benet's afsd.	William *Bennet,* 2d son, under age Aug. 1670. Benjamin Bennet, 3d son, under age Aug. 1670, living 29 Nov. 1723.	Sarah and Anne, both under age Aug. 1670; one of whom mar. (—) Pengrey and was living, as a widow, at St. Clement's Danes, 29 Nov. 1723.

Joseph *Bennet, a dry-* ⊤ (—)da. of *salter in London.* Query if not born in Brooke's buildings and bap. (as Thomas) 26 Feb. 1685/6 at St. Andrew's, Holborn; ? unmar. in 1708, but mar. before 1722; "living in debt Sep. 1734; died March 1741."

(—), mar. before 1722, "living Sep. 1734."

Alexander Bennet, *or Bennett, of Hatton Garden, Holborn, a merchant, who lived 9 years (1707-15) in the East Indies and brought thence a considerable fortune.* **Writer of the Diary.** "Born 25 Feb. 1688/9 in Essex street," St. Clement's Danes; died 30 Sep. and was bur. 6 Oct. 1759 at Dagenham, Essex, aged 70. M.I. Will dat. 7 Sep. and proved 21 Nov. 1759 in C.P.C.

Philip Bennet, living 29 Nov. 1723, "died 23 Dec. 1752."

Anne, living 29 Nov. 1723; either she or one of her sisters mar. (—) Burdett.[1]

Sources: Philip Morant's "The History and Antiquities of the County of Essex", vol 2, London, 1816, p. 107; "The Genealogist", new series, vol 20, London, 1904, p. 238

There is no evidence that I can find in the *London Gazette* for 1734 that Joseph was actually made bankrupt. According to the diary, he died in March 1741 aged fifty-six. So, if he was the father of our Samuel, he would have died seven months before the child was born. Alexander, according to his diary, also came to the rescue of his two brothers, John and Thomas, to save their places as Masters in Chancery, 'at great expense, after the South Sea year'. This was a financial crisis which hit Britain in 1720, in which thousands were ruined.

In an effort to learn more about the Essex family, I did follow up Joseph's two children, Philip and Anne. Philip was baptised at St Mary Abchurch, London, on 14 May 1716. His mother's name is given as Sarah. An elder sister, Anne (although her name is spelt Bennitt), was baptised at the same church three years earlier. Philip was a pupil at the Merchant Taylors' School.[11] This Philip Bennett, 'son of Joseph, gent of London', was, according to the school register, admitted sizar at Magdalene College, Cambridge at the age of seventeen. The term sizar was originally so called because a scholar received his commons, or sizes, free. It meant that an undergraduate was entitled to a slight remission of the ordinary fee in return for performing nominal services in the college. Philip went on to become a Fellow and a Proctor, and to be ordained.[12] He died in 1752.

Divorce a rarity

If Joseph's wife's name is given as Sarah, how can we ascend to him, when we know that our Joseph was married to a Jane? If this is the right Joseph, I can only conclude that Sarah died and Joseph made a late second marriage, perhaps shortly before his death. I am sure, incidentally, a divorce between Joseph and Sarah is ruled out. I have read that only 12 divorces were obtained by private Parliamentary bill during the whole of the 18th century. These divorces would have been granted only to people of considerable clout and influence. Jane might have been left to bring up the infant Samuel by herself. What could be more natural than for her to turn to her stepson Philip, newly ordained in 1740, for help and advice?

Philip's influence may have inspired Samuel to become a priest and also to take a Cambridge degree. Jane may have encouraged the young Samuel to return to Essex where he had family contacts and probably some goodwill.

Philip does seem to have had his lighter side: I obtained from the Pepys Library at Magdalene, Cambridge a photocopy of a long and wordy poem, *The Beau Philosopher*, written by him and published in 1736. Three years earlier he produced a farce called *The Beau's Adventures.* He also produced a collection of sermons which have not survived. His school, Merchant Taylors', does seem to have been favoured by the Bennett family, for William Henry Bennett-Dampier, son of John William Bennett and grandson of George Peter, was also a pupil there. But then other members of the family also went to Westminster, as we shall see later.

I feel there is a certain amount of circumstantial but not conclusive evidence that this drysalter Joseph is the right one – the Wiltshire origins, the Westminster address, the Essex and Cambridge associations, even the legal background. My father, Derek Curtis-Bennett, in his book *Curtis*[13] about my grandfather, Sir Henry, refers to the fact that there had been no lawyers in the family 'for many generations' – implying that there *had* been at one time. In which case the family legend that our Bennetts came from Pythouse could mean through the Essex Bennetts.

Desperately seeking Joseph

Despite extensive searching, I have not yet been able to find the marriage certificate of the Joseph and Jane Bennett shown on Samuel BD's ordination papers, nor Joseph's baptismal certificate, nor any will made by him. We do not know Jane's maiden name. Perhaps one day mention of the baptismal and marriage certificates will appear on the International Genealogical Index (IGI) when their research widens. There are plenty of Joseph Bennetts in 18th-century London recorded in IGI records, but no proof that any is the one for whom we are looking. I have even searched the records of 'clandestine marriages', of which there were thousands between 1700 and 1754 – to no avail. The children of these marriages were legitimate.

The archivist at Westminster Abbey library, where Samuel's baptism is recorded, told me that the words 'base born' would have been added if he had been illegitimate, and the father's name would probably not have been mentioned. I can find no record of Samuel Bennett in the bastardy depositions for St Margaret's of the relevant period. According to the church law at the time, he could not have subsequently been ordained if he had been illegitimate.

However, before the Marriage Act of 1753 uncertainty of proof dominated the marriage relationship. Marriages did not have to be performed in church, by a clergyman of the Church of England or according to the rites of the Book of Common Prayer. The free consent of both spouses, not the formal solemnities pronounced by a priest, was deemed to be the sole essence of marriage. A valid and binding marriage could therefore be created by an exchange of vows, witnessed by two persons.

As for Joseph's will, I have looked in the most obvious places – the Prerogative Court of Canterbury at the Public Record Office, and also in the lesser archdeaconry, consistory and peculiar courts at Lambeth Palace and the Greater London Record Office, without any success.

Bennett, which is the middle-English diminutive of Benedict, is an exceedingly popular name, in England and in its variations overseas. There are many different spellings which I have learnt to disregard. A Joseph Bennet is recorded in the burial register for St Margaret's, Westminster on 18 March 1749. This could be our man. He was buried in an unmarked grave in the cemetery, in the area which is now grassed over. The Churchwardens' Accounts at the Westminster Archives Centre show that the total cost of the funeral was 8s. 6d. – 2s. 6d. for the ground, 2s. 10d. for the knell, 3s. for the cloth and 2d. for the parson! It is indeed difficult to pinpoint our Joseph Bennett. However, there could be some other Joseph lurking around of whom as yet we have no knowledge.

Killed by cricket or tennis ball?

Are there are other clues to the identity of our Joseph, the one actually shown on Samuel BD's ordination papers? Yes, indeed. One pertinent fact emerges in all the family papers and especially in the family bible: Joseph met an untimely death, killed either by a cricket or a (real) tennis ball. The family bible names King George I or II as the thrower of the fatal ball; other sources say Joseph was playing tennis with the Prince Regent at the time.

This is a very persistent legend, appearing in all the family pedigrees that I have seen, including those emanating from collateral branches. About this alleged accident: George I died in 1727, long before the birth of BD; the Prince Regent was born in 1762, long after we presume Joseph to have died. Oddly enough, Frederick, Prince of Wales, son of George II, died of pleurisy in 1751 as the result of a blow from a ball while playing cricket at his home at Cliveden. Again, the blow is sometimes attributed to a tennis ball.

George II (1683-1760), however, did show an interest in the game, for he is known to have attended matches at Richmond and Kew. Cricket was played at Tothill Fields, the cricket ground of both Westminster residents and the pupils of Westminster School in the mid-18th century. Joseph's son, Samuel BD, was almost certainly a pupil at the school. Family legend asserts this, and in the *Records of Old Westminster School*[14] there is listed a Bennet who was a pupil at the school in 1754. Samuel would then have been 13, exactly the right age to enter. Is it not possible that Joseph perished during a parents' match, or was struck as a bystander by a carelessly thrown ball? It has been known for people to be killed by a ball striking them in the chest. A report in *The Times*[15] suggested that if the chest wall is struck at the moment when the heart muscle is at its most relaxed, the blow can trigger an extra heart beat which can then lead to cardiac arrhythmia, collapse and death. According to John Goulstone, an authority writing on cricket in the *Genealogists' Magazine*,[16] there were two well-known cricketers called Bennet, known as Little and Tall Bennet, in mid-18th-century London. But I can find no connection with Joseph here.

Summary of evidence

If I have to come down on one side or the other in this matter, I would slightly bet on sailor Sam Benett of the Norton Benett family being the father of Joseph. This is partly because I find Dick Dampier-Bennett's letter to Jack Benett a revealing piece of evidence, and because of the insistence of all pedigrees and papers that I have seen that we did indeed emanate from Pythouse, or rather from Wiltshire.

I find it hard to believe that this family legend is entirely without foundation, especially as George Peter Bennett, a clergyman, appears to have believed it and must have got his information from somewhere. What is strange is that our particular family has always spelt the name 'Bennett' and indeed since Edwardian times, as far as I can tell, has used the crest of the Pythouse coat of arms – a Cornish chough on a whelk shell, with the motto *Mihi Consulit Deus* (The Lord counsels me). Why did the descendants of DD – George Peter and Percy in particular – adopt this crest when in

4 The Bennett of Pythouse crest on mourning envelope used by Emily, Lady Curtis-Bennett.

fact the original crest of the Norton Bavant Benetts[17] might be the more appropriate one? I can only think that perhaps my great-grandfather, Sir Henry Curtis Bennett, who seems to be the first one to have worn a signet ring bearing the Pythouse crest, influenced his cousins to do the same. There is also the fact that Sir Henry married a woman with a rather more distinguished and established ancestry than his at a time when there was a revival of interest in genealogy. He presumably could have established his own coat of arms when he was knighted in 1913, but he died almost immediately afterwards, and his two sons seem not to have bothered.

As I have already mentioned, the spelling of the surname is irrelevant and one should ignore the variations. Spelling was not standardised until the mid-17th century. I have even found the name spelt in different ways in the same document. So we could belong to the Bennett, Benett, Bennet or even Benet family. If any of the family theories of ancestry is right, our Ben(n)etts probably never lived in the Pythouse which stands today, but in the Elizabethan building which preceded it.

Notes

1   GL MS 10326/98.
2   First edition (Harrison, 1842) and 2nd edition (1884), p.71.
3   *Church Times*, 12 May 1933.
4   E. Walford, *County Families of the United Kingdom* (R. Hardwicke, 1868), p.74.
5   R.E.M. Peach, *The Life and Times of Ralph Allen* (D. Nutt, 1895), pp.207-10 (Bath Lending Library).
6   R.C. Hoare, *Modern History of South Wiltshire* (J.B. Nicholas and J.G. Nicholas, 1829), vol.5, p.78.
7   *Merchants and Merchandise in 17th century Bristol* (Bristol Record Society, 1955), vol.19, p.253.
8   Privately circulated.
9   Richard Ellman, *James Joyce* (Oxford University Press, revised edition, 1982), pp.423-7, 459.
10 *The Genealogist*, new series (G. Bell & Sons, 1904), vol.20, pp.145-54, 238-9.
11 1561-1934, A-K, published at the school (1936), vol.1.
12 J.A. Venn, *Alumni Cantabrigienses*, Part 1 to 1751, vol.1, A-C (Cambridge University Press, 1922), p.134.
13 Derek Curtis-Bennett and Roland Wild, *Curtis* (Cassell, 1937), p.4.
14 *Records of Old Westminster School* (Chiswick Press, 1928), vol.1, p.73.
15 24 August 1995.
16 16 March 1994, p.769.
17 Fox-Davies, *Armorial Families* (Hurst and Blackett, 7th edition, 1929), vol.1, p.133.

To the Right Reverend Father in God Richard, by divine Permission, Lord Bishop of London, Greeting:

Whereas our well-beloved in Christ Samuel Bennett hath declared to us his Intention of offering himself a Candidate for the sacred Office of a Deacon, and for that End hath requested of us Letters Testimonial of his Learning and good Behaviour: We therefore, whose Names are hereunto subscribed, do testify that the said Samuel Bennett having been personally known to us for the Space of three Years last past, hath during that Time lived piously, soberly, and honestly, and diligently applied himself to his Studies; nor hath he at any Time (as far as we know or have heard) maintained, or written any Thing contrary to the Doctrine or Discipline of the Church of England; and moreover, we think him a Person worthy to be admitted to the sacred Order of Deacon. In Witness whereof we have hereunto set our Hands this ninth Day of February in the Year of our Lord, one Thousand seven Hundred and sixty seven.

John Tindal Rector of Chelmsford
John Stisted Vicar of Little Baddow
Charles Gretton Rector of Springfield-Bosvile in Essex
H Chalmers Rector of Little Waltham
Wm Master Rector of East Hanningfield
E Hatton
Waltham
Caspr Molineux

5 Local clergy back Samuel BD's desire for ordination.

PART 2

MOSTLY MEN OF THE CLOTH

Samuel Bennett, BD, friend of Oliver Goldsmith; Samuel, DD, prison reformer, then embassy chaplain; George Peter Bennett, back to Essex; Owen Dampier-Bennett, Dean of Nassau; Augustus Frederick Bennett, Congregational minister, his prolific family; Reginald Bennett, the 'horizon seeker'

Enigmatic Samuel BD

The details about the early life of Samuel BD, Joseph Bennett's son, are very sketchy and he has about him the quality of an orphan. It is curious that nowhere in any family papers is there any definite information about his parentage, except a few references to the shadowy Joseph. There is a big gap between Samuel's birth in 1741 and his appearance aged 25 at St Mary's Church, Broomfield, Essex on 1 February 1767 when he announced during divine service that he intended to be a candidate for Holy Orders. Where was he during those lost years? BD probably learnt his fine handwriting (as demonstrated in his meticulous parish records) at Westminster School. Some of his descendants were also educated at the school; for instance, his great-grandson, John William Bennett.

One pedigree I found, also in Jack Benett's papers, claims that Samuel 'lived in Abingdon Street with two old aunts from Wiltshire' – just round the corner from the school. Abingdon Street, opposite the Houses of Parliament, used to contain Georgian houses which survived until World War Two (WW2). The houses were pulled down in the '60s and replaced by an open space, now known as Abingdon Green, with vistas of the Abbey and Parliament. MPs are frequently seen being interviewed by television reporters in this area today. I have searched the rate books for that period and can find no record of the Misses Bennett as inhabitants of Abingdon Street, or Lindsay Lane, as it was called until about 1750. I did find references to a Bennet Street and a Bennets Court in the same vicinity, as well as Bennet's Yard. Other family papers claim that Samuel lived in Great George Street, Westminster.

A Thomas Benett of Norton Bavant, who could be related to Samuel, was also a Westminster pupil, entering the school in 1744 at the age of fifteen. Thomas, the son of Thomas Benett and Etheldred Wake (see Chart 4), went on to become High Sheriff of Wiltshire and a Registrar of the Prerogative Court of Canterbury, a probate court of the Archbishop of Canterbury. A person of obvious influence, he could have befriended young Samuel BD although a later pupil, and guided him towards the church.

Both putative Bennett homes – Great George Street and Abingdon Street – were not far from St James's Westminster, now better known as St James's, Piccadilly, a fine Wren church consecrated in 1684. The rector from 1729-33 was Dr. Robert Tyrwhitt, Canon of Windsor, Canon Residentiary of St Paul's and Archdeacon of London. His wife was a daughter of the Bishop of London: Mr. Tyrwhitt was therefore a powerful figure. His eldest son was Thomas Tyrwhitt, the celebrated classical commentator.[1] The second son, Edmund Tyrwhitt, prebendary of St Paul's from 1756-88, was vicar of Broomfield at the very moment when BD made his declaration there in 1767. It therefore seems reasonable to assume that BD met this family in Westminster and was offered some kind of job by Edmund, perhaps tutoring his children, of whom there were several.

I have searched Broomfield, but can find no record of BD or his family living there. St Mary's, Broomfield dates from Norman times and boasts one of the six round towers to be seen in the county. Edmund Tyrwhitt, according to a pamphlet I picked up there, obtained £200 from Queen Anne's Bounty to supplement the incumbent's stipend. Another vicar was Philip Morant, the famous Essex historian. BD must have been residing in the neighbourhood for at least three years before his ordination, as a whole raft of local clergy signed a testimonial on 9 February 1767 saying that they had known him for three years while he was pursuing his studies. One of the signatories, Charles Laval Molineux, a Norfolk vicar, had also been at Westminster School.

There were no theological colleges in those days, so even graduates had to undergo some further training before they were ordained. During those three years and before, BD could have been part of the household of the local landowner, Robert Haselfoot, who witnessed his marriage certificate. Another witness at BD's wedding was John Steffe, vicar of Little Baddow, who seems generally to have taken BD under his wing. He signed a document offering BD the job as curate in his parish on 7 February 1767 – several weeks before BD was ordained deacon on 15 March 1767 at the Chapel Royal, Whitehall. He was priested on 14 June of the same year and in the same place. It seems significant that BD was ordained deacon and priest with a gap of only three

6 Broomfield church, Essex.

months between each ceremony. A gap of a year or more is usual, and there must be special circumstances for a departure from this custom.

Judging by the number of clerics, headed by the Rector of Chelmsford, who signed his application to become a deacon, every effort was made to help him fulfil his vocation and further his training. So BD settled down to a lifetime's ministry in what was still part of the diocese of London. A country living then represented absolute security, with no retirement age, a freehold, glebe rents, Easter offerings and fees, and would have been especially attractive to someone with an insecure family background and little money. So 1767 was BD's *annus mirabilis.* During that year he was ordained deacon and priest, became curate of Little Baddow, then Boreham, and married the local vicar's daughter, Mary Butterfield, on 1 October 1767 by licence. BD was curate of the nearby parishes of Hatfield Peverel and Ulting concurrently with Boreham. He became vicar of the charming, bijou riverside church in Ulting in 1770 and in Hatfield Peverel in 1775.

Mistress of William the Conqueror

The original Hatfield Peverel Priory, of which the church forms a part, was founded by Ingelrica, the wife of Ranulph Peverel, a Norman knight whose name is on the roll of Battle Abbey. She had been the mistress of William the Conqueror and wished to atone for the errors of her early life. Her recumbent effigy lies on the window sill in the north aisle. The Priory was dissolved by Henry VIII in 1538, but most of the buildings escaped destruction. The estate was bought by John Wright in 1764. Today Hatfield Peverel is a commuter village for people working in London and elsewhere. Indeed, Little Baddow, Broomfield, Kelvedon and Writtle – all places where the Bennetts held benefices – are now considered most desirable dormitory areas for people working in the capital.

Samuel's entry in *Alumni Cantabrigienses* is puzzling, as it puts his date of entry to Emmanuel College, Cambridge as 1778 at the age of twenty-four. An explanation for this has been suggested to me by Dr. Simeran Gell, college archivist. She surmises that BD took advantage of the Elizabethan 'ten year rule' which stipulated that a man must be older than 24 to be entitled to automatic conferral of a degree after being on the college books for ten years. BD therefore went onto the college books in 1778, when he was thirty-seven. We know from other records[2] that he graduated in 1788 with a *Sacrae Theologiae Baccalaureus* (Bachelor of Divinity) degree. Dr. Gell reveals that BD gave his county of origin as Middlesex, but unfortunately there is no mention of his parents in the admission register. What is certain is that BD was not well off, because – like Philip Bennett before him – he entered college as a sizar. However, the practice of having to perform menial tasks around the college had lapsed by that time. BD's decision to pursue a Cambridge degree in 1778 and choice of college may have been influenced by his brother-in-law, James Butterfield, who was admitted sizar at Emmanuel on 14 February 1766.

I have found in Lambeth Palace Library[3] a Bishop's Visitation return made by BD in 1790, in which he reports that 'parents are not much disposed to send their children to be catechised as I could wish, I usually catechise in Lent'. Catechising, now consigned to history, was for centuries the accepted way of inculcating Christian teaching, chiefly into the young. BD also states that there were no papists in the parishes and few dissenters. This reflects the hostility which was felt towards both groups of people at that particular time. BD complains about money in a letter dated 1 November 1810 to the Bishop of London.[4] BD moans about the smallness of his income, only £13 6s. 8d. a year, plus £25 contributed by a charitable person. 'After repairs to the property, a very small sum remains to the vicar,' he writes. He also says that he has held this post for 20 years without the aid of a curate, and was the first vicar to have kept house, with a family, in the parish. Happily, as recorded in the Visitation of 1815, the stipend was increased, thanks to a Parliamentary grant of £50, to almost £90 per annum.

BD encouraged young Samuel and Samuel's two older sisters to take part in parish affairs, and they sometimes signed marriage registers, even at a tender age. One early marriage register, dated 9 November 1767, is of particular interest. BD had shortly been married himself. One of the witnesses at the wedding between a Thomas Chapman and Martha Fuller he conducted on that November day was none other than … Joseph Bennett.

John Watkins, my Australian cousin and mentor, thinks that there is a strong possibility that this was BD's father, and I see the logic of his reasoning. It is possible that Joseph could have been in Essex to attend his son's wedding two weeks earlier. This Joseph Bennett could be the Joseph Bennet, gentleman, who was living in Castle Yard in 1774, according to page 9 of the Westminster Poll Book of that year.[5]

Friend of Oliver Goldsmith

BD died in 1823 at the age of 81, and is buried in the nave of St Andrew's, Hatfield Peverel, where he was vicar for 48 years. DD's memorial tablet to him in the church (and also at All Saints', Ulting) refers to his 'kind and beloved father'. John Watkins reports in *Dear Descendants* that the *Essex Chronicle* in May 1823 described the scene at his funeral as follows: 'The solemn scene made a deep impression on the minds of a numerous and respectable assemblage of persons'. The report referred to BD as 'a truly venerable and much-respected clergyman … his memory will ever be held in affection and esteem by his parishioners'. BD's will was a very short and simple affair. He left everything to his son, Samuel, with a few bequests to his daughter, Mary Anne and a grandson. There is no mention of any family heirlooms left him by his father, which again does suggest that he began life in rather impoverished circumstances.

I had always imagined that poor BD led rather a lonely life after his wife died in 1775 aged 27, giving birth to their only son. However, perhaps he was not as solitary as I thought. When clearing out the attic in my mother's house in West Sussex in 1993 I came across a strange leaflet giving a brief outline of the life of BD's grandson, the Revd. George Peter Bennett, vicar of St Mary the Virgin, Kelvedon. It refers to BD as 'a man of great erudition, the intimate friend of Oliver Goldsmith and other celebrities of the day'. Goldsmith was a successful poet, playwright and essayist

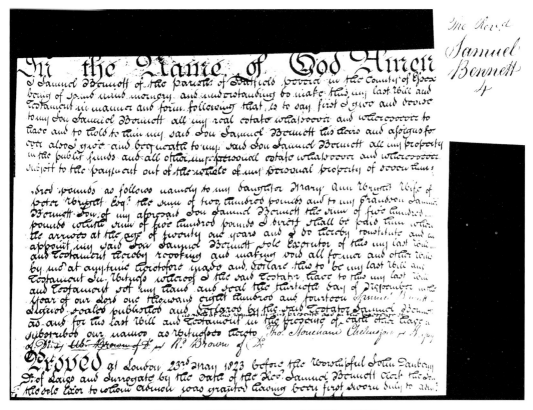

7   Samuel BD's will, proved 23 May 1823.

and friend of Johnson and Garrick. How he kept in close touch with BD living in Essex in days of difficult transport is not easy to imagine. The portrait I possess of BD painted towards the end of his life shows a man with a high forehead, a rather melancholy expression but a touch of humour about the mouth. What did he, in his Essex backwater, know of the great events of his time? What did he think about the French Revolution and the Napoleonic threat? Did he ever hear the music of Mozart or read the poetry of Byron? We shall never know.

Samuel Bennett DD, prison reformer, then embassy chaplain

Whereas his father, and indeed his son, George Peter, my great-great-grandfather, spent all their lives in Essex parishes, Samuel DD exhibited a restless spirit and ventured further afield. Like his father, he was a graduate of Cambridge. He was at Peterhouse (the oldest college in Cambridge) and later 'migrated' to Queens' College.

He was ordained priest, also in the Chapel Royal, London, in 1800 and on 1 October 1801 married 15-year-old Mary Ann Craneis at Writtle, Essex. This 800-year-old church had just suffered a catastrophe. In April 1800, the tower collapsed, bringing down the bells and demolishing a cottage nearby. The restoration was not completed until 1802, but services continued as normal in the intervening period. After being curate at Writtle, DD's first vicarship in 1804 was at an Essex parish,

Great Wakering. At this time he was studying for his doctorate in Divinity, which he was finally awarded in 1823, after preaching a sermon in Latin at Cambridge University church. However, he had a bad start at Great Wakering, for no house was available for him. For a while he and his wife were living in Writtle, presumably with his in-laws, Robert and Sarah Craneis. In letters to Bishop Porteus of London[6] in 1806 we find him saying that he, his wife and his daughter, Mary Ann, had all been suffering from the ague and bilious fever. He complains about the 'unwholesomeness of the country … the great and frequent fogs in the spring and autumn … the badness of the water', and blames them for the illness. A Dr. Badeley of Chelmsford wrote a medical certificate for him to the Bishop, commenting 'Mr. Bennett I believe to be a very worthy young man who has always exerted himself to the utmost to support his amiable wife'. DD tried at one point to persuade the Bishop to let him rent a house at Southend, but he settled in Great Wakering to raise his numerous family, which eventually comprised 11 children. He combined his clerical duties at Great Wakering with the chaplaincy of the barracks at Chelmsford, and also took in pupils to augment his income.

Perhaps his work as a chaplain stood him in good stead, for in 1816 the Bishop of London recommended DD to be the first chaplain in charge of the new General Penitentiary at Millbank. A salary of £400 a year with a house went with this. DD continued to be vicar of Great Wakering until 1822, so presumably left the parish in the hands of a curate. This was the age of plurality in the Church of England and the custom of having several livings at the same time was widely practised.

The family moved to Millbank, so DD returned to the London of his father's youth – and escaped the fogs of Essex. Millbank, on the site of what is now the Tate Gallery, was Britain's first attempt at making a prison a place of reform and rehabilitation rather than merely a place of punishment, embodying principles expounded by Jeremy Bentham.

The prison was in the shape of a six-pointed star and covered seven acres of low-lying marshy ground near the river. It was a cold, gloomy building with labyrinthine passages, and was the largest prison in London, used for men and women awaiting transportation or referral. Prisoners were confined to separate cells and made shoes and mail bags. They were forbidden to communicate with each other for the first half of their sentence. The locality and the diet were extremely unhealthy and in 1822-23 epidemics of scurvy and cholera affected half the inmates, killing 30 of them. Hardly the most salubrious environment in which to bring up a young family.

The Education of Criminals

The Bennetts' eighth, ninth and tenth offspring were born while the family lived at Millbank. August Frederick, the youngest son, tells how DD would relate to his family 'with a peculiar zest' the revelations made to him by noted burglars of the day.[7] DD was praised for his work in the first annual report to Parliament in 1817 for the 'great proficiency which has been made, under his direction, in reading and writing and in religious and moral instruction'. DD believed very strongly in education for criminals, as he showed in a sermon he preached at Bishop's Stortford and which was reported in local newspapers.[8] In it, he spoke about 'some of the pathetic cases' he had come across. They included a young man who had helped thieves break into his master's warehouse and was sentenced to death; this was commuted to transportation for seven years. Another young man, twice in prison, totally destitute and covered in rags, was given decent clothing, work was procured and he subsequently found himself in a 'comfortable position'. Another youth, son of 'a most respectable gentleman', convicted of embezzling property belonging to his employers, was pardoned by the King after four years.

'This young man is now a partner in a respectable house abroad and is in the constant habit of corresponding with me,' said DD. 'As a proof of his gratitude, he not long since sent me a most affectionate letter, accompanied by a handsome gift of plate.'

DD concluded:

Among the numerous convicts that have come under my knowledge, I have found but few who have been instructed in the National or Sunday schools. It is not among the pupils of these schools that the race of hardened profligates are trained, who have startled our courts of justice and made wise men tremble for the safety of the age. Let those who doubt the necessity of the religious education of the poor visit the dreary abodes of our prisons – let them inquire of the unfortunate objects within their walls and they will find that a large portion of the inhabitants are those who have never been educated and among these must be classed the most hardened and desperate. And even among those who could read or write I could soon discern a most lamentable ignorance of moral and religious duties – yes, many as ignorant of the first principles of religion as the wildest savage.

8   St Peter's, Walton-on-the-Hill, Surrey. The church contains a Norman lead font and a chained bible. (Drawing by Keith Charles.)

In 1822 DD left Essex for good and became rector of St Peter's, an attractive, flint church at Walton-on-the-Hill in Surrey, straddling the old Pilgrims' Way from Winchester to Canterbury. He continued to work at Millbank, but found it very hard going in the last years there. In April 1823 we find him writing to the Bishop of London[9] about a 'severe and alarming illness' in the Penitentiary and 'scenes of misery and distress'. He claimed to be often summoned from his bed at night to administer to patients. 'I certainly suffered from anxiety and fatigue, so much so that I was fearful my health would not be preserved … I think the duty almost too hazardous for anyone who has so large a family as mine,' he wrote. He asked for another job in the London diocese, so that he could be near his father – who in fact died that very year. DD stuck it out for another couple of years, finally resigning in March 1825, after 'nearly ten years of a most laborious, hazardous and unprecedented service'. By 1847, the Millbank reformatory experiment had failed. It became an assessment centre for candidates for transportation, ending its days as a women's prison in 1890. It was finally demolished in 1893. The site was cleared and work began on the new Tate Gallery.

While at Millbank, the Bennett family had become friendly with Augustus Frederick, Duke of Sussex, uncle to Queen Victoria. The Duke and other members of the Royal Family were interested in the social experiment, and DD became the Duke's honorary chaplain. On one occasion DD dandled the future Queen Victoria on his knee while visiting the Duke at Kensington Palace. The Duke became godparent to Augustus Frederick Bennett (1826-94) from whom John Watkins of Melbourne, Geoffrey Bennett of Oxted, Nancy Robinson Flannery (née Noon) of Adelaide and Meredith Roden (née Bennett) of Wisconsin, USA, are descended (see Chart 6).

There is a theory, as expressed in John Watkins' *Dear Descendants*, that the Duke was the father of Augustus Frederick by Mary Ann Bennett, DD's eldest daughter, who later married James Renshaw. The birth of the boy was not registered until he was 22 months old, and there were other odd variations to the usual procedures. Mary Ann, apparently, took full charge of Augustus Frederick. The theory does explain DD's desire to live abroad and the dates fit in well with the Bennetts' forthcoming 'exile' to Caen and, as we shall now see, even further afield. Incidentally, the Renshaws' great-grandson, Charles, married Jean Beauchamp who was the sister of Katherine Mansfield, the writer (see Chart 1).

Caen and Constantinople

In June 1828 DD wrote again to the Bishop[10] from Walton-on-the Hill, referring to the ill-health which had been experienced by his family the previous winter because of the 'severe coldness' (was he a hypochondriac, I ask myself?). He announced his intention to live abroad, and to receive under his care the sons of English gentlemen. He and his wife Mary had already made an exploratory trip to France, he said, to 'inquire into prospects in English churches in large towns', and had been to church in Calais. Another motive, DD admitted, was to add to his 'very limited' income. Non-residency was granted by the Bishop of Winchester and in 1829 the family moved to Caen where DD was appointed chaplain. He reported back to London[11] that he was doing his best to get on with his Roman Catholic counterpart. 'I am treated with much civility and respect', wrote DD. 'The number of people attending church increases, there were 60-70 at the last communion. I've never met a more decent congregation.'[12]

The youngest Bennett son, Augustus Frederick, remembers having to flee during the Revolution in the reign of Charles X; and meeting the British Consul at that time, none other than Beau Brummel. He was the dandy who had been banished from the English court by George IV for being too familiar. Beau Brummel would say to any

1 (3) AUGUSTUS FREDERICK BENNETT 1826 - 1894
. +Harriet Allbon 1834 - 1921
...... 2 Frederic George Bennett 1858 - 1922
.... +Ellen Kate Helmore 1851 - 1916
.... 3 Violet Bennett 1890 - 1961
.... +Cedric William Lyon Noon 1895 - 1960
.... 4 David Lyon Noon 1926 -
.... +Nerida Kathleen Laver
.... 4 NANCY ELIZABETH NOON 1929 -
.... +David Robinson 1928 - 1984
...... 2 Dr. John Henry Bennett 1860 - 1934
.... +Amelia Gardner
.... 3 Ernest Leslie Bennett 1887 - 1980
.... +Alice Emily Geraldine Bennett
.... 4 Meredith Leslie Bennett 1921 -
.... +Richard Wood-Taylor 1920 -
.... 3 Dr. Frederick John Bennett 1889 - 1952
.... +Doris Mercy Willmott
.... 4 Dr. John Willmott Bennett 1924 -
.... 4 Dr. Winfield Robert Curtis Bennett 1927 - 1994
.... +Elmira Lumaye Mary Rachel Murray
...... 2 (Andrew) Percy Bennett, CMG 1866 - 1943
.... +Winifred Youell 1876 - Unknown
.... 3 Iris Winifred Bennett 1900 - Unknown
.... +Richard Wyndham
.... 4 Joan Olivia Wyndham 1921 -
.... +Maurice Rowdon 1922 -
.... *2nd Husband of Joan Olivia Wyndham:
.... +Alexander Shivarg 1923 -
...... 2 Reginald Allbon Bennett, OBE 1878 - 1945
.... +Beatrice Brown 1893 - 1981
.... 3 Frederic Wilson Bennett 1925 -
.... +Margaret Hallett
.... 4 Freya Bennett 1958 -
.... +Jeremy Wilkinson
.... 4 Martin William Bennett 1960 -
.... +Avril Southern
.... 4 Clyde Torquil Bennett 1964 -
.... +Amanda Taylor
.... 3 GEOFFREY LEGRAND BENNETT 1926 -
.... +Sheelah Susanne Humphreys
.... 4 Roger Anthony Bennett 1957 -
.... +Irene Gasde
.... *2nd Wife of Roger Anthony Bennett:
.... +Mary-Jo Schneider
.... 4 Colin Michael Bennett 1958 -
.... 4 Nigel Timothy Bennett 1965 -
.... +Beate Iris Kierspe 1964 -
...... 2 Edith Daisy Bennett 1879 - 1963
.... +Arthur Albert Watkins 1881 - 1965
.... 3 JOHN LESLIE WATKINS, OBE 1911 -
.... +Natalie Gertrude Carey 1914 - 1965
.... 4 Margaret Anne Watkins 1937 -
.... +John Michael Lester
.... 4 Natalie Jane Watkins 1939 -
.... +Clifford Walter Bills
.... 4 Ian Carey Watkins 1943 -
.... +Caroline Gail Bride
.... 4 Phillip Arthur Watkins 1944 -
.... +Denise Rosemary Wilson
.... 4 Lucinda Josephine Watkins 1949 -
.... +Daryll George Alfred Malsead

CHART 6

Some of the
Revd. Augustus Frederick Bennett's
nearly 150 descendants

Percy Bennett, CMG

Sources: family papers of John Watkins of Melbourne and
Geoffrey Bennett of Oxted; "The Life of a Christian
Minister", A.F. Bennett, 1890; "Reminiscences connected
with my official career, 1893-1927, Percy Bennett, CMG.

friend who called and saw a score of cravats lying on the floor: 'These are our failures'. Brummel eventually died penniless in Caen. After three years, DD resigned the chaplaincy at Caen, returning to Walton via diligence, sailing ship and coach.

In 1835, at the age of 60, DD, his wife and some of his young children ventured even further afield – to Constantinople, where he was to be chaplain to the British Embassy, at a stipend of £250 per annum. Until WW1 there were only five British embassies in the world, and Constantinople, known as the 'sublime port', was one of them. DD was certainly keen to have the Constantinople appointment, as is revealed in a letter to him from Bishop Blomfield of London of 31 October 1835[13] when DD had been in Constantinople for just a few months. It appears that DD was less than satisfied with the appointment. The Bishop refers to 'the situation which you were so anxious to obtain'. Perhaps DD was dismayed to find no English church there. The British Ambassador, Lord Ponsonby, told him not to trouble to hold any services as only he and his wife would form the congregation. Most of the household, he said, were Roman Catholic or Greek Orthodox. The further implication of the Bishop's letter was that DD was considering resigning because the stipend was so poor. When he was told by the Bishop that the Government would not pay his expenses home, he appears to have changed his mind about returning to England.

A romantic if melancholic nature

Augustus Frederick gives many details of the family's life in Constantinople in his book. DD, he says, was a 'great pedestrian' generally carrying with him St John's Gospel and 'meditating upon its contents with evident delight'. DD copied out by hand a selection of his favourite passages from French and English literature in an anthology which he gave to his daughter Emily 'from her affectionate father'. It now belongs to Geoffrey Bennett, his great-grandson, who kindly lent it to me. The dedication in the book reads: 'Our fathers find their graves in our short memories and sadly tell us how we shall be buried in our survivors'. Further on in the book he writes: 'Let me be found in the Registry of God, not in the record of man'. DD contributed a touching poem of his own composition written as a tribute to another daughter, Henrietta. She died in Malta in 1841 *en route* to Marseilles to be married. DD also lost his fourth son, Joseph, born in 1818. He went to the Lebanon to work in a silk factory but died of the 'Palestine fever' while on a visit to the Holy Land. No wonder perhaps that DD displays a romantic, if somewhat melancholic nature in his choice of prose and poetry for this volume. The name Joseph does not appear again in the family tree, as far as I know.

One of the family papers says that before going to Turkey DD was offered the Bishopric of Bangor (before the Province of Wales was created), but turned it down because of failing health. In that case it seems a strange choice to go to Turkey, where the plague was endemic. But perhaps he thought the warm climate would do him and his family good. DD informed the Bishop of London that the British Embassy in Constantinople badly needed a chapel. He succeeded in persuading the British Government to build one in the grounds of the British Embassy, the first English church in

Constantinople. It was unfortunately destroyed in a great fire which raged through the city in the year of DD's death at 72 in 1847. According to John Watkins, a small oil painting of the original chapel hangs in the study of the chaplaincy house of what is now the British Consulate General (the Embassy having transferred to Ankara).

DD had a cosmopolitan attitude and got on with all nationalities. Among those who followed his funeral procession were about 200 mourners – English, French, Swiss, Greeks, Armenians, Jews and many of the inhabitants of Pera (the Christian suburb of Constantinople), as well as representatives of the diplomatic community, 'so greatly was the deceased Chaplain respected'.[14] DD was buried in the English cemetery at Pera, but his grave is no longer visible. John Watkins tried to find it on a visit to Turkey some years ago.

Meanwhile, what of BD's two daughters? The elder daughter, Elizabeth, never married, and presumably acted as housekeeper to her father. She pre-deceased him by 12 years and is buried in the same grave in the nave of Hatfield Peverel church. The younger girl, Mary Anne, married into a well-known Essex family, the Luards. There is a large file of material on the Luards in the Chelmsford record office, which I have been through, without finding anything illuminating to our search. Actually Peter Luard, Mary Anne's husband, took his mother's name, Wright, by royal licence, in compliance with the will of his grandfather, John Wright. It was this John Wright who was the patron of the living at Hatfield Peverel, where BD was vicar for so many years.

George Peter Bennett, Vicar of Kelvedon

George Peter Bennett, elder brother of Augustus Frederick, entered the Church like his father and grandfather before him. Both of them seem to have had money worries all their lives. No wonder, then, that George Peter seized the chance to marry some-one with some prospects when the opportunity presented itself. He married Charlotte Curtis, daughter of a prosperous Dorking doctor, in 1834 in St Martin's, Dorking, the church where she had been christened in 1811. I assume that George Peter met his future bride when he was living at Walton-on-the-Hill, Surrey when his father was rector there. George Peter entered Peterhouse, Cambridge in 1828. Unlike his father and grandfather, he was admitted 'pens' which meant that he did not have to perform menial tasks around the college. He 'migrated' to St Catharine's in 1830, graduating in Divinity in 1833 and was ordained to the priesthood two years later.

It was in this year that the same Bishop Blomfield of London, who was in correspondence with his father, recommended him as curate to the Revd. J. Bannister of Wickham St Paul's, Essex, describing George Peter as 'a very suitable and diligent young man for whom I am desirous on his father's account to obtain a curacy'.[15] On leaving this curacy in 1835, George Peter was presented with a silver sugar bowl which I now possess. It bears an inscription from the parishioners, saying the present is 'a token of their esteem and affection for his faithfulness and charity in the discharge of his sacred duties'.

George Peter spent four years as military chaplain at Weedon barracks in Northants from 1846-50, and there was a spot of trouble during his time there. I haven't been able to discover quite what it was, but there are hints in letters to him from the Bishop of London.[16] He wrote to George Peter on 7 April 1848 saying: 'No blame is imputable to you, although you were perhaps a little wanting in that knowledge of the world which would have put you on your guard against the threats of unscrupulous men.' The Army records at the PRO give no indication what the trouble was. I can only assume that George Peter had some problem with unruly or threatening soldiers. This problem, whatever it was, does not seem to have affected his career, for shortly afterwards he was appointed vicar of White Notley, Essex, where he remained for the next nine years.

Eventually he settled down as vicar of Kelvedon for the next 32 years. The modern village probably lies on the site of the Roman town of Canonium, according to the great art and architecture historian, Nikolaus Pevsner, who says that excavations have produced a Roman kiln, pottery and coins.[17] George Peter and Charlotte, who died in 1894 – three years after her husband – are both buried near the church door. There is an account of the vicar in the *Essex Herald*[18] describing him within a few days of his death 'being drawn in his bath-chair down the village street in order that he might bid what he felt was a last adieu to some of those to whom he had long ministered'.

The *Essex Herald* also reports that, during George Peter's tenure of the living, the church had been completely restored, the bells retuned and rehung, a new chiming

9   Interior of St Mary's, Kelvedon. The Curtis-Bennetts have a family plot in the graveyard.

clock placed in the tower, the burial ground twice enlarged and a new organ installed. There is also mention of his character in the same obituary notice: 'As a teacher and speaker Mr Bennett possessed an earnestness of manner and an impressiveness of delivery which always made themselves felt upon his hearers and lent force to his remarks … he was a man of simple tastes and habits with a tenacious memory, which he retained fully up to the last'. According to *Alumni Cantabrigienses*[19] and the Peterhouse Admission Book,[20] George Peter was the author of *Sermons* and *Addresses to Soldiers* – but these I have been unable to locate.

George Peter's eldest son, John William (whose descendants became known as the Dampier-Bennetts and the Bennett-Dampiers) also became an Anglican clergyman. After attending the family university – Cambridge – where he was at Emmanuel College, John William eventually became vicar of St Paul's, Hampstead for more than 20 years. He was one of the first incumbents of modern times to introduce oratorio services with full orchestral accompaniments in a London church. He was one of the pioneers of the Gregorian movement and for many years acted as precentor to the London Gregorian Choral Association at the annual festivals held at St Paul's Cathedral. Owen, his son and one-time Dean of Nassau, married my parents. I have a dim memory of visiting Owen's house in west London and watching him playing billiards. He was apparently a formidable mixer of cocktails.

Augustus Frederick Bennett, Congregational Minister

The descendants of AFB, as his prolific family call him, are well documented in John Watkins' book, *Dear Descendants*. AFB eventually returned to England from Turkey to become a Congregational minister. But many of his descendants, perhaps inspired by Samuel DD's wanderlust, roamed the world and now live overseas: John Watkins, although born in Scotland, has lived in Australia since 1913, had a distinguished career in aviation and has at least 23 descendants; Nancy Robinson Flannery (née Noon), author and archivist, lives a busy life in Adelaide with her present husband; Meredith Roden (née Bennett) is based in Fond Du Lac, Wisconsin with her husband, Francis; and Geoffrey Bennett, a geophysicist, spent many years devoted to oil exploration in many countries including Australia, India, Burma, Nigeria and Europe. Of his three sons, Colin and Nigel have also found careers in the oil industry; Roger, the eldest, moved to the USA and has set up his own painting and decorating business.

Reginald Bennett, the 'horizon seeker'

Geoffrey's father, Reginald, led an extraordinary and adventurous life, always on the move. He sometimes referred to himself as a 'horizon seeker'. In 1903 he was appointed British Resident Officer in the Colonial Service in Kudat, British North Borneo. Repeated bouts of malaria caused his resignation. During WW1 he was assigned to the Military Intelligence Section of the Home Office and for his work there, mainly in the ports of South Wales, he was awarded the OBE. In 1920 he joined Thomas Cook & Son and for the next two decades he travelled the world as their representative. Undaunted at having reached the age of 63 during WW2, he joined the RAF based in Liverpool to undertake special intelligence duties. Worn out by this arduous work, he died in 1945 just before the end of the war.

Reference notes

[1] *Dictionary of National Biography*, vol.19, p.1,373.

[2] J. Smith, *Graduati Cantabrigienses, 1659-1823* (Cambridge, 1823), p.40.

[3] *Fulham Papers*, Porteus, microfilm, 38 and 40.

[4] *Ibid.*, Randolph, vol.1, f.87.

[5] British local history section, Institute of Historical Research, University of London.

[6] *Fulham Papers*, Porteus, vol.1, ff.117-26.

[7] A.F. Bennett, *The Life of a Christian Minister* (J. Crampton, Sawston, 1890), p.14.

[8] *Fulham Papers*, Howley, vol.7, ff.119-33.

[9] *Ibid.*

[10] *Ibid.*

[11] *Ibid.*, Blomfield, vol.65, f.101.

[12] *Ibid.*

[13] *Ibid.*, vol.2, f.22 (microfiche).

[14] A.F. Bennett, *op.cit.*, p.136.

[15] *Fulham Papers*, Blomfield, vol.6, f.1.

[16] *Ibid.*, vol.46, f.36 and vol.47, f.60.

[17] *The Buildings of England (Essex)* (Penguin Books, 2nd edition, 1965), p.255.

[18] 4 August 1891.

[19] 1752-1900, p.230.

[20] 1615-1911, T.A. Walker, p.433.

PART 3

THE BENNETTS GO DOUBLE-BARRELLED

Sir Henry Curtis Bennett, JP, scourge of the suffragettes; Sir Henry Honywood Curtis-Bennett, a fashionable KC; Derek Curtis-Bennett, QC, defender of 'Lord Haw-Haw'; Susan, Deirdre and David Curtis-Bennett; Sir Noel Curtis-Bennett, founder of National Playing Fields Association; Virginia Gallico, lady-in-waiting to the Grimaldis

Henry Curtis Bennett, target of the suffragettes

George Peter's second son, Henry, decided the law was for him. Unlike his father and elder brother, he did not go to Cambridge (perhaps there was not enough money), but was educated at Kelvedon.[1] A handsome man from his photographs, he was frequently likened in appearance to Lord Asquith, the Liberal Prime Minister. Henry is chiefly remembered for being one of the first magistrates to deal with militant suffragettes. Members of the Pankhurst family came before him at least three times for public order offences. In 1907 at Westminster police court he sentenced the two Pankhurst daughters, Christabel and Sylvia, to prison for 14 days each for 'disgraceful street scenes'. The following year, Mrs. Emmeline Pankhurst and Christabel were sent to Holloway for three months and 10 weeks respectively as inciters to riot. In 1912 at Bow Street Mrs. Pankhurst came before him again, with 123 other women who had been arrested for window-smashing.

10 Cartoon of Sir Henry Curtis Bennett (1846-1913), London magistrate (*The Throne and Country*, 29 August 1908).

STARTLING DISCLOSURES OF ALLEGED SUFFRAGETTE PLANS.

Seven Suffragette leaders and two men were charged at Bow Street Police Court yesterday with conspiring with Emmeline and Christabel Pankhurst and other members of the Women's Social and Political Union to cause damage contrary to the Malicious Damage Act of 1861. Among the defendants were Mrs. Drummond, general organiser, and Miss Annie Kenney, organiser of the W.S.P.U., the manager of the firm which printed this week's issue of the "Suffragette," and a chemist. Startling disclosures of alleged militant plans were made. 1. Suffragettes try to sell the "Suffragette" outside Bow Street Police Court. 2. Mr. Curtis Bennett arrives at the court. 3. Detective-inspectors Hawkins (left) and Fowler, who were concerned in the raid. 4. Princess Duleep Singh talks to sister Suffragettes at Bow Street.

THREE SUFFRAGETTE LEADERS ELECT TO GO TO PRISON FOR THEIR CAUSE.

SIR CURTIS BENNETT, T[

"We will go to prison," was the defiant declaration of Mrs. Pankhurst at Bow-street on Saturday, when Mr. Curtis Bennett ordered the three suffragette leaders to promise to be of good behaviour for a year, or, in default, go to gaol for periods ranging from ten weeks to three months.—(*Daily Mirror* photographs.) (1) The magistrate. (2) Miss Pankhurst (standing), Mrs. Drummond (in centre), and Mrs. Pankhurst in the dock.

A detective followed him abo[
Only a week after receiving his knighthood [
dead. He was leaving the platform after at[

11 Members of the militant Women's Social and Political Union, including the Pankhursts, came before London magistrate Sir Henry Curtis Bennett for public order offences on several occasions. He was subsequently sent an anonymous bomb in a cigarbox and after that was guarded by detectives.

SUFFRAGETTE BOMB
SENT BY POST.

ATTEMPT TO KILL THE CHIEF LONDON MAGISTRATE.

INFERNAL MACHINES IN A TRAIN.

YESTERDAY'S OUTRAGES.

Bomb sent by post to Mr. Curtis Bennett, the chief London magistrate.

Attempt to wreck a Kingston train by means of three bombs.

Highlands, a large mansion at Wes Folkestone, set on fire. Damag £1,000.

Organ at Penn parish church, Buckin hamshire, destroyed by fire.

A bomb attempt on Mr. Curtis Ben the chief London magistrate, is the mad act of the r nant women. not been for th lance of the the bomb, wh tained bulle nearly a qua pound of gu and was through would have livered to Bennett a yesterday was dis the case against the suffragette leaders.

The bomb was so constructed that a considerable explosion, entailing loss of life or

Mr. CURTIS BENNETT

BOMB AT BOW-ST.
MAGISTRATE'S LIFE IMPERILLED.
NARROW ESCAPE.
HOW MILITANT FUNDS ARE SPENT.

But for the vigilance of the police, a bomb sent through the post would have been delivered to Mr. Curtis Bennett, the chief magistrate, at Bow-street, yesterday at the very time that he was engaged in hearing the charges against the suffragette leaders. Although subsequent investigation showed that the mere unwrapping of the brown paper which enclosed the object would not have caused an explosion, the bomb was so constructed that its effects would have been deadly had it been dropped or struck. The stamping of the postmark might easily have ignited the powder, and had the parcel been flung carelessly from one sorter to another and dropped there would have been disastrous results.

The parcel, about 5in. long and 2in. wide, was delivered at the entrance to the court at 11.30 a.m. It was simply addressed in what looked like a feminine hand to "Mr. Curtis Bennett, Bow-street Police Court," and in the left hand corner was the word "Immediate." The officer who received it noticed that it was unusually heavy, and, suspicion being aroused, it was at once dropped into a pail of water. Afterwards the parcel was found to be a tobacco tin wrapped round with wire. The lid was fitted on the top, and driven through it was a nail, at the end of which a percussion cap was fitted. The tin was full to the top of gunpowder and shot, into which the nail penetrated to some depth. The shot apparently consisted of the contents of cartridges. Had the bomb burst its effects, in the view of the police, would have been deadly. Supposing it had come into the hands of Mr. Curtis Bennett, the consequences would have been very serious if he had let it drop. The marvel is that when the Post Office people stamped it an explosion was not caused. The words "Votes for women" were written on paper inside the

D MAGISTRATE, DROPS DEAD IN FRONT OF THE LORD MAYOR A WEEK AFTER RECEIVING HIS KNIGHTHOOD.

him from suffragettes.   Going to Bow-street.   The officers cycled behind his carriage as he drove to and from the Court.

Curtis Bennett, the Metropolitan Chief Magistrate, is | and died in the Lord Mayor's parlour before two doctors, who were called, could arrive. The Lord Mayor broke the sad news Mansion House yesterday when he was seized with faintness, | to the Chief Magistrate's family. He was one of the first of the metropolitan magistrates to deal with the militant, and al detectives mounted on bicycles were told off to guard him from any attack by the suffragists.—*Daily Sketch* Photographs.

A *Times* report[2] records that damage worth £5,000 had been done. Mrs. Pankhurst said that, as soon as she was released from prison, she intended to go further, as far as was necessary, to show the Government that women intended to get representation for their taxes. She was given a two months' sentence on this occasion.

Henry had to deal with a number of other cases involving militant suffragettes and became the object of their hostility. They sent him a bomb disguised as a cigar-box, but happily it was discovered by suspicious officials at Bow Street. Another time he was walking (his hobbies were walking and reading) along the North Downs at Margate when he was attacked by two women who tried to hurl him over the cliff. For the last few months of his life, he was always followed by two detectives. I asked his daughter Muriel how he felt about votes for women. She replied that he felt it was his duty to uphold the law as it stood. So I do not know whether he was for or against in principle. However, as his obituary notices show, he was said to have a kindly and

12   Newspaper cutting on the sudden death of Sir Henry in 1913.

SUDDEN DEATH OF SIR H. CURTIS BENNETT.

Sir Henry Curtis Bennett, who was only recently appointed Chief Metropolitan Magistrate, was taken ill yesterday at the Mansion House after speaking at a meeting of the St. Giles' Christian Mission, and died shortly afterwards.   1. Sir Henry Curtis Bennett in court, and (2) arriving at Bow Street.

genial disposition and in general to be lenient with young, first-time offenders. He was represented in a 1970s television series on the suffragettes in which he showed concern about their welfare in prison.

Henry was knighted on 19 May 1913 on his appointment as Chief Metropolitan Magistrate. He died in a dramatic way of a heart attack on the following 2 June. He had been speaking at the Mansion House at a meeting of the St Giles' Christian mission, an institution which helped discharged prisoners, thus echoing his grandfather's concerns for criminals. He was shaking hands with the Lord Mayor of London when he fell, striking his head against a marble pillar. The application of a small bottle of brandy which he always carried with him did not revive him. There were many newspaper tributes to

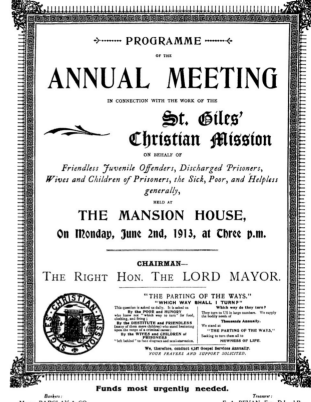

→ —— PROGRAMME —— ←

OF THE

ANNUAL MEETING

IN CONNECTION WITH THE WORK OF THE

St. Giles'
Christian Mission

ON BEHALF OF

Friendless Juvenile Offenders, Discharged Prisoners, Wives and Children of Prisoners, the Sick, Poor, and Helpless generally,

HELD AT

THE MANSION HOUSE,

On Monday, June 2nd, 1913, at Three p.m.

CHAIRMAN—

THE RIGHT HON. THE LORD MAYOR.

"THE PARTING OF THE WAYS."
"WHICH WAY SHALL I TURN?"

This question is asked us daily. It is asked us | Which way do they turn?
By the POOR and HUNGRY who know not "which way to turn" for food, clothing, and firing ; | They turn to US in large numbers. We supply the bodily needs of **Thousands Annually.**
By the DESTITUTE and FRIENDLESS (many of them mere children) who stand hesitating upon the verge of a criminal career ; | We stand at "THE PARTING OF THE WAYS," Seeking to turn them all to **NEWNESS OF LIFE.**
By the WIVES and CHILDREN of PRISONERS "left behind" to face disgrace and semi-starvation. |

We, therefore, conduct 4,387 Gospel Services Annually.
YOUR PRAYERS AND SUPPORT SOLICITED.

Funds most urgently needed.

Bankers : Messrs. BARCLAY & CO.   *Treasurer :* F. A. BEVAN, Esq., D.L., J.P.

13 Programme cover of the charity meeting at which he collapsed.

BUCKINGHAM PALACE

June 3rd 1913

Dear Lady Bennett,
    The King is distressed to know of the grievous sorrow which has so suddenly befallen you and desires me to convey to you the expression of his true sympathy. It was only as it were a few days ago that the King knighted Sir Henry Curtis Bennett when His Majesty much enjoyed an interesting conversation with him and was so much pleased with the interview —
Believe me
Yours very truly
Stamfordham

14 Letter from Buckingham Palace expressing sympathy for his widow.

him at the time of his death, referring to him as 'a man with a genial temperament and a charming smile'. The stress occasioned by the suffragette cases may have had something to do with his death at the age of sixty-seven. More than 100 wreaths were sent to his funeral at Kelvedon, where his widow, son Henry, daughter Muriel and grandson Derek are all buried. In the south aisle of the church, there is a stained glass window to Henry's memory, erected by his widow and three children. The subject of the window is the six works of mercy, as found in St Matthew 25, verses 35 and 36. The window was dedicated by the Bishop of Colchester on 1 November 1913. Muriel, a very devout lady, donated the money for a crucifix in the chapel in 1964.

15 *Carte de visite* showing Henry Curtis Bennett and Emily Hughes-Hallett on honeymoon.

Henry was married by his clergyman father to Emily Jane Hughes-Hallett, the daughter of a Kent solicitor, on 15 August 1878 at St Paul's Church, Hampstead. There is a rather charming note in the *Colchester Mercury and Essex Express*[3] of that year reporting that the couple had returned from their 'wedding tour' and had been greeted in Kelvedon by schoolchildren who cheered the happy couple. They followed the carriage to the vicarage, the gateway of which had been decorated with evergreens and the motto 'Welcome, Long Life, Health and Happiness'. The church bells rang a 'merry peal' in their honour and later the couple were given a drawing-room clock and candelabra from the inhabitants. This was the marriage which in particular brought new genes into the Bennett family, genes which perhaps spurred them on to greater ambitions in the future.

The Curtis-Bennetts' London home was at 118 Lexham Gardens, Kensington. I remember visiting Emily there in her widowhood. She was a very upright, dignified lady, holding an ebony stick and surrounded by Victorian knick-knacks. She provided a home for a rather fierce parrot and also for her daughter Muriel, who was reputed to suffer from a weak heart. The house was left to the younger son, Noel and was lived in by his widow Dorothy and son Paul until the middle 1980s. In the nearby St Philip's church in the Earl's Court Road, where Henry worshipped and regularly read the lesson for 26 years, there is a wall plaque to his memory, erected by his widow and children. It recalls that he was an alderman of the Royal Borough of Kensington.

Henry Honywood Curtis-Bennett, a fashionable KC

The second Sir Henry is probably the best known Curtis-Bennett, although his son, Derek, also had many sensational legal cases. A full account of the life of Henry (known to his family as Harry) can be found in the book written after his death by my father and Roland Wild.[4] Wild, who was at Radley College with Derek, was an adventurous character. He was a foreign correspondent who reported on the Spanish Civil War, drove in the Monte Carlo rally and crossed America in a caravan. In February 1946 he wrote a profile of Derek and Margot in *The Queen* magazine in which he commented on Derek's 'loathing of the countryside ... there is only one walk for Curtis-Bennett and that is across the park'.

16   Henry Curtis-Bennett (Harry) as Secret Service officer in World War One.

Sir Henry was one of the best-known criminal lawyers of his generation. Margot Curtis-Bennett, his son Derek's wife, told me that a hush would descend upon the court when Henry entered, followed by his clerk, Hollis, carrying his books and papers. He appeared for the defence in many celebrated cases of the era, notably for Mrs. Edith Thompson in the Thompson and Bywaters murder case, and for Lord de Clifford in a manslaughter case involving a car accident in 1935. This was the last occasion on which a peer was tried by his fellows in the House of Lords. He was acquitted.

Not so successful was the 1922 defence of Herbert Armstrong, the solicitor who was hanged for the murder of his wife. In 1997 there was a Channel 4 documentary, followed by a book, called *The Hay Poisoner*.[5] In both the presenter and author, Martin Beales, sought to prove that Armstrong was wrongly convicted. Beales refers to Henry as 'without doubt one of the most able advocates of the day', but also quotes a reference to him as 'a theatrical counsel and no great lawyer'. There is in Derek's book a photograph of Henry standing beside Sir Ernest Pollock, the Attorney General, a collateral ancestor of my

17 Harry was a favourite subject for cartoonists; he was portrayed in court and as an Indian elephant because of his ample girth and 'prodigious memory' (*The Bystander*, 15 January 1930). He was also depicted as a fearsome cross-examiner, and a newspaper diarist at an Eccentrics Club dinner imagined Harry's head on a coin, in the manner of a Roman emperor.

THE INDIAN ELEPHANT OR CURTIS BENNETT

GEORGE WHITELAW'S WHO'S ZOO—No. 7

Sir Henry Curtis-Bennett, K.C., who is this week's addition to George Whitelaw's Who's Zoo, is one of the most brilliant and successful men at the Bar. Like the elephant, in which guise he is seen above, Sir Henry is possessed of a prodigious memory—as many a witness has found to his cost, and ends!

HENRICUS IMPERATOR DIVUS

stepfather, David Pollock. Sir Ernest conducted the case for the prosecution against Armstrong.

Harry was a well-known personality about town. Although lean and trim in his youth – he won a cycling Blue at Cambridge – he acquired a love of good living, and was an habitué of the Colchester Oyster Feast (see plate 22). He was an early fan of the motor car, and loved to tour in France with his family. Derek and his wife, Margot, who spoke good French, often used to accompany him. Margot remembers attending Cup Final football matches with her father-in-law, and occasionally accompanying him to City dinners, when his second wife was not available to go with him. Because of his wit, Harry was much in demand as an after-dinner speaker, particularly at City functions. The result was that he put on a good deal of weight in days when this was not taken so seriously as it is today. The aquiline good looks of his youth gradually disappeared and, because of his girth, he became known as the Falstaff of the Bar.

Cross-examining Mata Hari

Harry was knighted in 1922 for his work in the Secret Service during WW1. He was attached to the War Office's Contra-Espionage department from 1916-17 and was employed by Scotland Yard to cross-examine suspected spies from 1917-19. These included Mata Hari, the most famous woman spy of the century. He was a Member of Parliament from 1924-26 representing Chelmsford, but applied for the Chiltern Hundreds when his wife sued him for divorce. Harry was not particularly at ease in the House of Commons, preferring the law courts. After the divorce, he married his long-time mistress, Mary Jeffries, from a Gloucestershire family, who outlived him by many years. They sailed to South America for their honeymoon and their arrival in Rio was remarked upon by the Brazilian press.

Like their father, Harry and his brother Noel both suffered from heart trouble, and also collapsed and died in public situations. Harry, who by then had been appointed Chairman of London Sessions, fell to the ground with a coronary thrombosis at the age of 57 while making a speech. This was at a dinner of the Greyhound Racing Society at the *Dorchester Hotel* in October 1936. Nearby him at that

18 Newspaper cutting on Harry's death.

41

Master
Sir Henry Curtis-Bennett, K.C.

Wardens
Arthur W. Jarratt
Col. H.P.L. Cart de Lafontaine, O.B.E., F.R.I.B.A.

Wardens
Alderman Sir Percy Vincent, J.P.
Norman L. Ball.

AMICITIAM TRAHIT AMOR

Sir

You are desired by the Master and Wardens of the Worshipful Company of **Gold & Silver Wyre Drawers** to be and appear upon Monday the Sixth day of January 1936 by 11.45 of the Clock in the fore-noon at **INNHOLDERS HALL** College Street, Cannon Street, in the City of London it being a Quarterly Court.

I am requested by the Master to say that he will be pleased if you will meet him at Luncheon immediately at the conclusion of the Court.

Please fill in and return the post card by return. (Past Masters will be so good as to wear their Badges)

33. Walbrook,
London. E.C.

A. Charles Knight Clerk

For Agenda see within.

19 Harry enjoyed many City contacts and was Master of the Gold & Silver Wyre Drawers' Company.

Sir Henry Honywood Curtis Bennett Knt Citizen Gold Silver Wyre Drawer of London was admitted into the Freedom aforesaid and made the Declaration required by Law in the Mayoralty of Sir Charles Henry Collett, Knt., Mayor and Sir Adrian Donald Wilde Pollock, Knt., Chamberlain and is entered in the book signed with the Letter S.2 relating to the Purchasing of Freedoms and the Admissions of Freemen (to wit) the 8th day of June in the 25th Year of the reign of King GEORGE V And in the Year of our Lord 1934 In Witness whereof the Seal of the Office of Chamberlain of the said City is hereunto affixed Dated in the Chamber of the Guildhall of the same City the day and Year aforesaid.

20 He was given the Freedom of the City of London in 1934.

moment was his brother, Noel, who was himself to die while addressing an audience at a charity dinner at the *Savoy Hotel* in December 1950. Harry's great friend, St John Hutchinson, KC, paying public tribute to him, said that in his opinion he was one of the least ostentatious people he had ever come across. Jeremy, the son of 'Hutch', as he was known in the family, was my father's pupil at the Bar. He was at one time married to the actress Peggy Ashcroft and later became Lord Hutchinson of Lullington.

During his lifetime Harry was lent Boreham Lodge, Essex by his mother who had inherited it from her husband. He had planned to live there when he retired. The house had once belonged to the Butterfield family, and there is still a Butterfield Road nearby. The house is just a few yards from the church where Thomas Butterfield, Samuel BD's father-in-law, was vicar. I well remember staying in the house as a child – the smell of wood as one entered the house and the watercress beds in the grounds. There was a dogs' cemetery where my grandfather's dogs, Judge and Jury, were buried. In Boreham, Harry is remembered locally for the donkey he kept in a field opposite the house. Good children were taken there to stroke it for a treat. The Revd. William Smith, a former vicar of St Andrew's, Boreham and author of an article on Harry in a book about the town,[6] writes that Harry is also remembered for his interest in cricket. For a number of years he cap-tained a Boreham eleven against a Min-istry of Health team brought down by his brother, Noel. At other times an eleven came from the CID.

Harry, always convivial, provided an excellent lunch on these occasions. The house was sold by auction after Harry's death in 1936, together with The Old Rectory and freehold building land. The sale papers refer to Boreham Lodge as 'an old world residence' occupying a 'very pleasant position enjoying fine open views over the surrounding country'. As was usual in those days, the house included a

21 Boreham Lodge, Essex, as it was in 1978. (Photo by the Revd. William Smith.)

22   Colchester Oyster feast, 17 October 1934. (Reproduced by courtesy of Colchester Borough Council.)

wine cupboard, housemaid's pantry, scullery and larder. There was an orchard, ornamental fish pond, thatched summer house, walled kitchen garden and pasture land comprising 14½ acres in all.

Ann, Harry's daughter, told me that in her childhood the family used to go on 'ancestor hunts' in Essex. A paragraph in *Curtis* states that 'the Bennett family sprang from the Benetts [*sic*] of Pythouse, Wilts, where they have lived since at least early in the 12th century'.[7] So this was evidently the firm belief of this generation too.

Derek Curtis-Bennett QC, following his father's footsteps

Harry's relationship with his son, Derek, was a dominant and complicated one. Derek, born on 29 February 1904, was obsessed with the idea of following in his father's footsteps. They went to the same prep school in Eastbourne, the same public school, Radley, occupied the same rooms at Trinity College, Cambridge, and took silk at the same age. Harry became a Bencher of Middle Temple Inn on the same day that Derek was called to the Bar. They also shared a love of cars. During our schooldays my sister Deirdre, brother David and I used to acquire great prestige when our parents arrived in a Rolls-Royce or Lagonda. It was either at his prep school or at Radley that Derek was given a school report which read: 'Owing to the charm of his manner it is impossible to resent the enormities he serves up as Latin prose'.

23   Harry (seen here with Elsie) was an enthusiastic early motorist.

45

24 & **25**   Derek as a pageboy … and with his mother and sister in Egypt.

Derek was rather successful at Cambridge, although gaining only a third in his finals (like his father). Perhaps he spent too much time on other activities – running with various university cross-country teams and writing sketches for the famous Footlights dramatic club. One of his contributions, 'A Peep at Justice', was described in a local newspaper report as 'a clever police court skit, the action of which is alleged to take place in a town with the suggestive name of Camford'. Derek's mother used to say that he had wanted to go into the Navy, but he was prevented from doing so because his eyesight was not good enough. So he followed his father's example and became a barrister, specialising in criminal work.

Derek also had many big criminal cases. Among his most famous were William Joyce ('Lord Haw-Haw'), hanged for treason in 1946, Christie, the Notting Hill murderer and Klaus Fuchs, the atom spy. Derek had two dramatic international cases during his career: the first was in 1947 when he flew to Rangoon by flying boat to defend U Saw, the former Prime Minister of Burma, who was accused of abetment in the murder of the then Prime Minister, Aung San, and six members of his Cabinet. Aung San was a nationalist leader, and the shooting took place in the Council Chamber shortly after the first Anglo-Burmese peace talks with Clement Attlee. U Saw disclaimed any knowledge of the murders, which were carried out by his underlings. Derek was engaged for the defence because U Saw's brother was living in London at the time, looked for a good criminal lawyer with a big name and settled on my father.

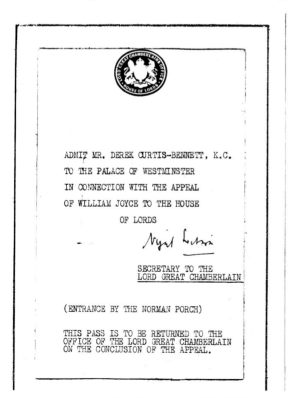

26   Mementoes of the William Joyce ('Lord Haw-Haw') trial.

According to an account of the trial by a Burmese barrister who was present,[8] on 19 December Derek gave a 'brief, skilful and dignified address', during which he cited the murder of Thomas à Becket and suggested there might have been a parallel in this case. Unfortunately for U Saw, Derek's eloquence did not convince the special tribunal and, after an unsuccessful appeal, U Saw was hanged in the May of the following year. The case was a particularly stressful one for Derek. Many Burmese barristers refused to defend U Saw because of the tensions the murder had aroused in the country. Both the defence and the prosecution lawyers received police guards to protect them against angry crowds.

In the summer of 1997, 50 years after the assassination, BBC2 ran a programme called *Who really killed Aung San?* Using new witnesses, footage secretly filmed in Burma and recently de-classified British documents, the film examined evidence linking the assassination to shadowy British establishment figures. The evidence shown in the film, to my mind, was pretty flimsy, but it does raise the question as to why these facts did not come out at the time of the trial. More will surely eventually come to light on this subject.

27 & 28 Father and son outside court ... Sir Henry Curtis-Bennett with Sir Edward Marshall-Hall in 1923; Derek Curtis-Bennett arrives at a naval court martial with Jeremy Hutchinson in 1946 (photo: Planet News Agency).

He salted a gold mine

In 1950 Derek flew to South Africa to defend his Cambridge contemporary, Norbert Erleigh, against a charge of 'salting' a gold mine. This involved adding gold to a sample from a borehole, in an attempt to add to the potential value of the mine. Erleigh too was convicted, though I believe that Derek succeeded in getting his sentence reduced. The night before he went to prison for five years Erleigh, a prominent and popular figure in the social and sporting life of Johannesburg, appeared at a ball in white tie and tails, danced away quite cheerfully, greeting everybody with the words: 'See you when I come out'.

29 & 30   Four generations twice: *(above)* Frederick Hughes-Hallett, daughter Emily Curtis-Bennett, her son Henry Curtis-Bennett and Derek Curtis-Bennett; *(below)* Emily, Henry, Derek and the author, Susan Curtis-Bennett.

Derek had a quieter but no less effective court presence than his father. Courtroom style had changed by then to one of less flamboyance. I was sitting behind him in court on the day that the two Princesses, Elizabeth and Margaret, slipped in to listen to the case as part of their education in English institutions. He was appointed Recorder of Tenterden in Kent and also of Guildford in Surrey. My sister, brother and I, placed in the jury box, sometimes used to watch him hearing cases. Derek was a kindly and loving father, an intellectual who loved classical music (he used to play Beethoven while reading his barrister's briefs), literature and the theatre, especially the plays of Shakespeare. After the war he took us to many great performances on the English stage at the Old Vic. We saw Gielgud's *Hamlet* (and met the actor backstage) and Olivier's *Richard III.*

Derek was friendly with people like the author Charles Morgan, whom he advised with technical details for his 1947 novel *The Judge's Story.* I remember once

going to a Christmas party at Charles Morgan's house in Campden Hill Square, where every house had candles in the window. Derek enjoyed playing games like mahjong, bagatelle, Monopoly and poker with us. He was a big clubman, belonging to the Garrick, Travellers' and Beefsteak, founded in 1735 to celebrate 'Beef and Liberty'. At one of these clubs – the Beefsteak, I think – there was a famous dispute with the writer Evelyn Waugh, who had reputedly ill-treated a waiter. All the waiters there were called Charles. My father, as a member of the committee, had to remonstrate with Waugh. I rather took Waugh's side, protesting that he was a genius, and therefore ought to be forgiven.

As a diabetic, Derek was not called up in WW2, but did his share of fire-watching in the Temple. My mother remembers that on these occasions she was left to sleep on a camp bed in the basement of the *Savoy Hotel*. One night she found herself next to Ivor Novello, the actor and impresario. My parents, brother, sister and I were in London for some of the bombing raids. At one stage we all moved into the *Dorchester Hotel*. It was thought to be very safe because it was one of the few concrete buildings in London. It was ironic that next door in Deanery Street was a house, the lease of which had been left to my parents by my grandfather. We were never able to live there because it was riddled with dry rot. The family had some rather bitter things to say about the Church Commissioners, who owned the freehold. After the war the house was pulled down, and I believe that the Brazilian Consulate now stands on the site.

Many happy years

My father and mother enjoyed many happy years together, but were divorced in 1949. He had begun to drink heavily, and his sad and lonely death from asphyxia at the early age of 52 haunts us still. He was a sensitive man and took his work very much to heart. Perhaps the comparisons with his father were a perpetual burden to him. Like his father, Derek was married a second time, to a young girl called Janet Farquhar Rusk who tragically took her own life shortly before he was found dead in his flat in Kensington in July 1956.

An obituary note in *The Times*[9] said:

Derek's was essentially a kind and affectionate nature: he was always ready to befriend the young and inexperienced; and there was no man to whom family ties meant more ... many will mourn him, but not least those of us who were his colleagues of the Circuit and Sessions, where his personality had made so great a mark.

A particularly agreeable reference to my grandfather – and indeed all three legal Curtis-Bennetts – was made by the Judge, Sir Travers Humphreys in his book *Criminal Days*.[10] Reflecting that Harry was an admirable defender of prisoners, an excellent motorist, a genial *bon viveur*, but not the best student of the law, he wrote:

As he had a popular and successful father, Sir Henry Curtis Bennett, who became Chief Magistrate of the Metropolis, so he had a popular and successful son, Derek, now a KC, who by no means despises the law by which he makes his living.

I was born on 23 June 1929 in Charleville Mansions, Charleville Road, west London, in the same street as my father, Derek, I in a mansion flat, he in a house. My sister, Deirdre Elsie Elizabeth, was born in Wellington Square, Chelsea on 19 December 1933 and my brother, David Dangar Henry Honywood, at Campden Grove, Kensington on 22 December 1936 (see Chart 2). We spent our childhood in London, except for periods during WW2, when my parents rented various furnished houses in the country. Deirdre and I were educated at Westonbirt School, Tetbury, Gloucestershire, and I graduated in Moral Sciences from Girton College, Cambridge. David was educated at Radley College and served his National Service as a 2nd Lieutenant in the Life Guards. In 1955, Deirdre married James Townshend Boscawen, a grandson of the Duke of Montrose and great-grandson of the Duke of Hamilton. Deirdre and Jim had two children, Caroline and Diana, and five grandchildren by these two daughters. Jim died at the early age of 59, much mourned by all his family. In January 1998 Deirdre married a neighbouring widower, Sir John Drinkwater QC at Fairford church in Gloucestershire. In 1962 my brother David married Caroline Hubbard,

31 & 32 *(left)* Deirdre Elsie Elizabeth Curtis-Bennett as a 'girl with pearls' in *Country Life* (27 January 1955) following her engagement to James (Jim) Boscawen; *(right)* Jim and Deirdre Boscawen at their Perthshire home in the 1980s.

Photo: Ursy Burnand

33   1962 wedding of David Curtis-Bennett and Caroline Hubbard at St Paul's, Knightbridge.

34   Mark and Victoria Curtis-Bennett in Kensington Gardens, London.

whose maternal family, Grimston, claims descent from one of William the Conqueror's sword-bearers. They are the parents of Mark and Victoria and grandparents of two boys by Victoria. David and Caroline were divorced and in 1986 he married Frances Chaston (née Wolfenden) in the Seychelles where he lives and works. Caroline married Sir Bruce MacPhail, Managing-Director of P&O. Both my sister's and brother's first weddings took place in St Paul's, Knightsbridge. I married Peter Donald Rowland Senn (a journalist who won a history exhibition to St Catherine's College, Oxford) at Chelsea Old Church in 1955. We were also divorced.

Sir Noel Curtis-Bennett, civil servant and sporting enthusiast

Noel, the younger son of Henry and Emily (Chart 7), did not, like his father and brother, go to the family university. He was educated at Tonbridge, and was originally destined for the Church. Preferring an outdoor life, he worked first as a land agent on an earl's 5,000-acre estate in Worcestershire. He organised his first sports team there among the estate employees. In 1905 this led to a job as an Inspector at the Board of Agriculture and Fisheries. In 1920 he transferred to the Ministry of Health and finally in 1930 to the Treasury where he was an Assistant Secretary. Noel did a great deal to promote sport in Britain, helping to set up the Civil Service Sports Council, the Civil Service Motoring Association (CSMA) where he was president for 17 years and the National Playing Fields Association which has provided playing facilities for thousands of young people. At a complimentary dinner given in his honour by the Civil Service in 1928, tribute was paid to the work he had done in encouraging sports facilities, and reference was made to his 'magnetic personality, persuasive speech and spirit of camaraderie'. In 1937 the Guild of Master Motorists presented him with a trophy which he passed onto the CSMA, who renamed their annual road rally after him. He sat on many committees connected with sport, including the International Olympic Committee.

In his capacity as Organising Secretary to the Coalfields Distress Fund, Noel encouraged the then Prince of Wales, patron of the Fund, to visit South Wales, and was with the Prince when he made the famous remark: 'Something must be done'. These and other activities brought Noel into frequent contact with the Royal Family, and he was awarded the CVO in 1926 and the KCVO in 1932. Both were the personal gifts of the sovereign. It was King George V who gave Noel the sobriquet

"Hon. Treasurer"

Sir Noel Curtis-Bennett, K.C.V.O.

35 & 36 Sir Noel Curtis-Bennett, KCVO (1882-1950) as a country gent in 1905 ... and as Hon. Treasurer of the National Playing Fields Association.

37   Noel (hatless) with two monarchs: Kings George V and VI.

'the man who made Whitehall matey'. Besides a love of sport Noel had, in common with his brother Harry, an enthusiasm for acting. They took part in amateur dramatics as young men, and Noel became Chairman of the Civil Service Dramatic Society. As I have said, Noel died while making a speech at a charity function at the *Savoy Hotel* in 1950. His ashes were scattered over the Civil Service sports ground at Chiswick.

Noel's only son, Paul, was educated at Hurstpierpoint. He then entered Christ's College, Cambridge, where he read law, was President of the Cambridge Union and a member of the Cambridge Liberal Club. He served in the Navy during WW2, and was called to the Bar in 1950. He joined chambers in Brick Court and later in Hare

CHART 7

Sir Noel Curtis-Bennett,
distinguished civil servant

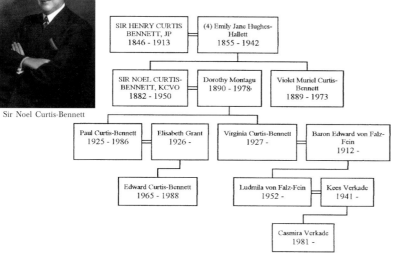

Sir Noel Curtis-Bennett

| SIR HENRY CURTIS BENNETT, JP 1846 - 1913 | (4) Emily Jane Hughes-Hallett 1855 - 1942 |

| SIR NOEL CURTIS-BENNETT, KCVO 1882 - 1950 | Dorothy Montagu 1890 - 1978 | Violet Muriel Curtis-Bennett 1889 - 1973 |

| Paul Curtis-Bennett 1925 - 1986 | Elisabeth Grant 1926 - | Virginia Curtis-Bennett 1927 - | Baron Edward von Falz-Fein 1912 - |

| Edward Curtis-Bennett 1965 - 1988 | Ludmila von Falz-Fein 1952 - | Kees Verkade 1941 - |

| Casmira Verkade 1981 - |

Sources: family papers and pedigrees; "Who Was Who" 1941-50; Civil Service Motoring Association; other Civil Service sources; profile in "Good Housekeeping" magazine, February 1940

Casmira Verkade, Virginia Curtis-Bennett and Ludmila von Falz-Fein (left to right)

Court in the Temple, with a mixed common law practice. He was eventually appointed a deputy county court judge. He died of heart trouble in 1986 while convalescing at Osborne House, Isle of Wight, and is buried in the cemetery at St Mildred's, Whippingham. This church, Rhenish-Gothic in style, was designed by Prince Albert and contains a Battenberg chapel. A splendid memorial evening to Paul was held in the Parliament Chamber at Inner Temple Hall by his friends and colleagues, who paid tribute to his sparkling conversation and intellectual gifts. His only son, Edward, by his second wife, Elisabeth Grant, died tragically in his early twenties.

38 Barrister Paul Curtis-Bennett (1924-86) escorts Serena Goode to her wedding to Robert Ballin at Holy Trinity, Brompton, London in 1975.

Paul's sister, Virginia, educated at Roedean, was married firstly to Baron Edward von Falz-Fein, a white Russian who settled in Liechtenstein, and after that to Paul Gallico, the American writer. They lived in Antibes in the south of France, and Virginia has been close to the Grimaldi family of Monaco for many years. Her daughter Ludmila by her first marriage lives in Monaco with her sculptor husband, Kees Verkade, and daughter Casmira.

Violet Muriel, born in 1889, was Henry and Noel's younger sister. She never married and devoted herself to her mother after her father's death. Despite suffering from the family heart trouble, she lived to the ripe old age of eighty-three. Her high-church funeral service was held at St Stephen's, Gloucester Road, South Kensington and she was buried in the family vault at Kelvedon by the Revd. Peter Elers, the then vicar. His name came into the news a few years later when he became the first President of the Lesbian and Gay Christian Movement.

Notes

1   *Who Was Who, 1897-1915*, p.57.
2   4 March 1912.
3   5 October 1878.
4   Curtis-Bennett and Wild, *op.cit.*
5   Martin Beales, *The Hay Poisoner* (Robert Hale, 1997).
6   E. Burgess (ed.), *More about Boreham* (The Lavenham Press, 1996), pp.204-5.
7   Curtis-Bennett and Wild, *op.cit.*, p.4.
8   Maung Maung, *Trial in Burma – the assassination of Aung San*, (M. Nijhoff, The Hague, 1963).
9   27 July 1956.
10 Sir Travers Humphreys, *Criminal Days* (Hodder & Stoughton, 1946), p.101.

PART 4

ASCENDING SOME FEMALE LINES

William Butterfield, pikeman at Flodden Field; a Comyns connection?; John Curtis, a doctor in Dorking; the Hughes-Halletts; Sir James Hallett, jeweller to the King; the Dunmow Flitch; three Lord Mayors of London; a link with the Knatchbulls, the 'best family in Kent'; John Graham and the American Revolution; the Honywoods

William Butterfield, pikeman at Flodden Field

Some of our female lines are very worthwhile investigating. The family of Mary Butterfield, the bride of Samuel Bennett, BD came originally from Yorkshire. I was delighted to find, at the Society of Genealogists in London, a Butterfield pedigree stretching back to one William Butterfield who 'flourished' at Morton Banks in the parish of Bingley, in the old West Riding of Yorkshire. This pedigree (see Chart 8) was drawn up by Alexander W.D. Mitton, former Rouge Dragon Pursuivant of Arms, so I think we can take it as reliable. This William was one of 11 Morton men who followed the Earl of Clifford to the Battle of Flodden Field in 1513, fighting against my mother's ancestors, the Scots.[1] William was a pikeman, that band of men who were the backbone of the English army and forerunners of the British 'square'. Another, later Butterfield – Francis – was a great friend of Charlotte Brontë.

I located in the Public Record Office, then at Chancery Lane, the will (proved 1780) of Mary Butterfield's mother, another Mary. As a widow, she was allowed to dispose of her possessions. Her husband, Thomas Butterfield, a graduate of Trinity College, Cambridge and Archdeacon of Chelmsford, died in 1766. His grave – and that of his wife and of his daughter, Mary – are to be found in the nave of Boreham church where he was vicar.

A Comyns connection?

Samuel DD, Samuel BD's son, married a Mary Craneis. Was there a connection with Sir John Comyns, Lord Chief Baron of the Court of the Exchequer, and the builder of a famous stately home near Chelmsford called Hylands? There is a monument to Sir John, who came from Dagenham, in Writtle church, where DD and Mary Craneis were married in 1801 when she was fifteen. One of the family papers names Mary as granddaughter and co-heir of John Comyns Esq, nephew of Sir John Comyns. Another version suggests that it was Mary's maternal grandmother, Mrs. Sandford, who married Sir John, after her husband, Dr. Sandford DD, Rector of Chelmsford, died.

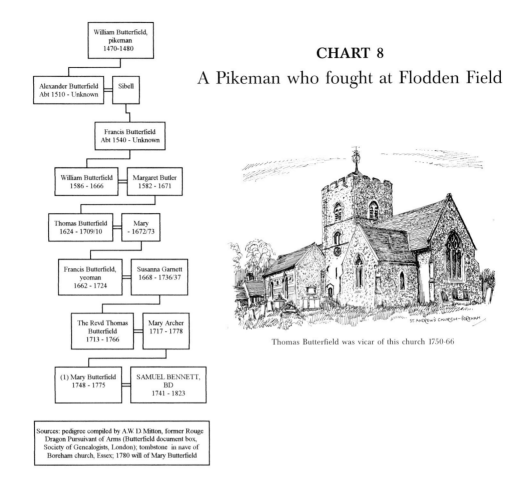

CHART 8
A Pikeman who fought at Flodden Field

William Butterfield, pikeman
1470-1480

Alexander Butterfield
Abt 1510 - Unknown — Sibell

Francis Butterfield
Abt 1540 - Unknown

William Butterfield
1586 - 1666 — Margaret Butler
1582 - 1671

Thomas Butterfield
1624 - 1709/10 — Mary
- 1672/73

Francis Butterfield, yeoman
1662 - 1724 — Susanna Garnett
1668 - 1736/37

The Revd Thomas Butterfield
1713 - 1766 — Mary Archer
1717 - 1778

(1) Mary Butterfield
1748 - 1775 — SAMUEL BENNETT, BD
1741 - 1823

Sources: pedigree compiled by A.W. D Mitton, former Rouge
Dragon Pursuivant of Arms (Butterfield document box,
Society of Genealogists, London); tombstone in nave of
Boreham church, Essex; 1780 will of Mary Butterfield

Thomas Butterfield was vicar of this church 1750-66

My great-aunt Muriel Curtis-Bennett told me that Judge Comyns was definitely a forebear. I even found an engraving of him among the family papers. Unfortunately Muriel died before I could get more details from her. In any case, Mary could only have been a direct descendant of Judge Comyns' father and brother. Stephen Foreman in his book *Hylands – the story of an Essex country house and its owners*[2] says that Sir John did marry three times, but none of his wives was called Sandford. Mr. Foreman confirms a strange coincidence: Elizabeth Hallett, daughter of James Hallett, an ancestor of my great-grandmother Emily Hughes-Hallett, married John Comyns, Sir John's nephew, on 23 May 1740 in St Paul's Cathedral.[3] On his uncle's death, also in 1740, he inherited Hylands and all his uncle's legal papers. He also was a lawyer, a member of Lincoln's Inn.

John Curtis, a Doctor in Dorking

George Peter Bennett's wife, Charlotte, was the daughter of John Adee (a variation of Adam) Curtis. He was a surgeon, practising in Dorking for many years. Although born in London,[4] he must have moved to Dorking at an early age, for he married by licence Elizabeth Young, also of Dorking, in St Martin's Church on 13 November

1801. The marriage allegation in Lambeth Palace Library states that the pair came from the same parish. The accompanying bond describes John Curtis as a 'gentleman'. Elizabeth, I suspect, could have been one of the Youngs of nearby West Street, Dorking. They were prominent members of the United Reform Church there.

By 1851 John Curtis was living in South Street with an unmarried daughter, Eliza, and two granddaughters. He died aged 78 in Reading on 7 March 1852, suffering from gallstones. Present at his death, according to the death certificate, was Henry Charles Curtis, his son, also a surgeon who lived in West Street, Great Marlow with 'a groom and a house servant'.[5] Henry had a number of connections in Reading. He was a member of the Reading Pathological Society and had connections with the Royal Berkshire Hospital. He wrote several learned papers on cholera and congenital malformation.[6] Perhaps his father had travelled to Reading to hear him deliver a lecture. John Curtis is buried with his wife, who died in 1837 aged 58, and other children who died in early adulthood, in the family vault on the south side of St Martin's. The churchyard lies over the old Roman road. Inside the church in the belltower there is a wall plaque to John Adee Curtis junior, Charlotte's brother, an army surgeon who died in Aden.

The Royal College of Surgeons, which was founded during the 19th century, has no record of John Curtis; nor is he listed as an apprentice to the Barber-Surgeons' Company of London which preceded the college. The Royal Society of Physicians

39 John Adee Curtis's house in South Street, Dorking as it is today.

Parish or Township of *Dorking*		Ecclesiastical District of	City or Borough of	Town of *Dorking*		Village of

Name of Street, Place, or Road, and Name or No. of House	Name and Surname of each Person who abode in the house, on the Night of the 30th March, 1851	Relation to Head of Family	Condition	Age of		Rank, Profession, or Occupation	Where Born
				Males	Females		
South St	*John Adee Curtis*	*Head*	*Widr*	*77*		*Medical not practising*	*London*
	Eliza Curtis	*Daur*	*Un*		*40*		*Surrey Dorking*
	Amelia "	*Gd Dauer*			*11*	*Scholar*	*" "*
	Mary "	*do*			*8*	*do*	*" "*
	Harriott Daniels	*Servant*	*Un*		*23*	*Domestic Servant*	*Suffolk Sudbury*
	Emma Rose	*do*	*Un*		*20*	*do*	*Kent Hernehill*

40 1851 Census return showing members of the Curtis household in South Street, Dorking (Crown copyright, reproduced by kind permission of the Public Record Office, HO 107/1598, f 293).

has no trace of him either, nor does he appear to have studied at any of the British or Irish universities, nor at Leyden where many English-speaking students matriculated. Before the Medical Act of 1858, some medical practitioners outside London had just an academic training. Another son, George Curtis of Dorking, was certainly officially qualified and was in partnership with his father at one time. George became an MRCS and also a Licentiate of the Society of Apothecaries in 1829. He was the father of Canon Hubert Curtis, vicar of the Church of the Ascension, Balham Hill, who helped officiate at the funeral of Sir Henry Curtis Bennett in 1913. George was

41 Death certificate of John Adee Curtis (1775-1852) (The design of the Death certificate is Crown Copyright and is reproduced with the permission of the Controller of The Stationery Office).

a witness at the wedding of Henry Curtis Bennett and Emily Hughes-Hallett, so there was a continuing relationship between the two families.

The Curtis house in South Street (formerly Butter Hill), now occupied in the upper floors by the *Dorking Advertiser* and on the ground floor by a shoe shop and the Dorking Tyre Service,[7] was substantial. John Curtis owned four other houses, plus gardens and stables, dotted around the town.[8] His death is noted in the *Gentleman's Magazine* of 1852.[9] One of his properties was a freehold house in the High Street and he also held land on which a number of cottages were built. This is still known as Curtis Gardens. There is also a Curtis Road, now the site of an industrial estate. I am puzzled how he came by his money. His will, which is four pages long with three codicils and extremely legalistic, reveals that he did indeed possess a lot of property, not only in the Dorking area, but also at several addresses in central London. The will gives the name of his mother-in-law, Kezia Young, but I have not been able so far to progress sideways or backwards from her.

Charlotte and her sister Honor were left a hundred pounds each in their father's will. Charlotte and her sisters Eliza and Louisa were bequeathed ground rents and leasehold properties in Bryanston Square, Bryanston Place, Church Street, Copland Street, Princes Street, Salisbury Street and Lisson Grove – all in the W1 or NW8 districts of London – very valuable properties, one would think.

The mystery remains about the origins of John Curtis. I always understood from my father that my brother, sister and I were one-sixteenth Irish. Whether the family of John Curtis or that of his wife Elizabeth Young came from Ireland I do not know, but this seems to be a possibility. My grandfather, according to his daughter Ann, used to say that he had inherited from his (female) Irish ancestor 'the gift of the gab and eyes set in with an inky finger'.

The Hughes-Halletts

The first three male Curtis-Bennetts all married women whose pedigrees are well worth investigating. The first Sir Henry, as I have said, married Emily Jane Hughes-Hallett (Chart 9). I well remember meeting cousin John Hughes-Hallett at the 1953 Coronation Fleet Review when the Queen reviewed 200 British warships. He was then a Vice-Admiral and commanded the aircraft carrier *Eagle*. He had been naval commander of the 1942 Dieppe raid (for which he was awarded the DSO) in WW2 and played an important part in planning the Normandy invasion of 1944. His obituary notice[10] said that he was the chief naval planner of Operation Overlord and the first to suggest the use of the Mulberry Harbour for the Dieppe raid. He was a bachelor and a somewhat intimidating character. He had a brother, Charles, who was also a Vice-Admiral. Apparently during WW2 these two, who had the reputation for being rather forbidding, were known as Hughes-Hitler and Hughes-Himmler.

Another of Emily's cousins, Leslie Charles Hughes-Hallett, a diplomat, was married to Violet Mary who, I remember hearing in my childhood, kept snakes in the bath. This is confirmed by Michael Shea in his book *To Lie Abroad*.[11] He quotes an old

42   Emily Hughes-Hallett (1855-1942) in court dress.

colleague who, recalling the eccentricities of diplomatic wives, tells of a Mrs. Hughes-Hallett, wife of a Latin American ambassador. She, according to this source, kept snakes in the wardrobe of the guest room, telling the visitors of this only the next morning at breakfast. If she saw two members of staff or their wives conversing at cocktail parties, she would bear down on them crying in a portentous, Lady Bracknell voice: 'This is incest'.

Emily's father was Frederick of Brooke Place, Ashford, Kent. He was a solicitor, whose firm, Hallett & Co., Ashford's oldest legal practice, still exists in the town. On 28 December 1995 I visited the offices to attend the unveiling of a mahogany plaque naming all the firm's past partners. I saw there a large framed photo of Frederick with his second wife, sitting in a carriage with a dog. The firm used to specialise in looking after farmers. In the old days sheep and cattle were driven along Bank Street where the offices relocated from nearby North Street in the late 19th century. What a contrast to Ashford International today, the Eurostar gateway to Paris. One of the partners told me that the firm handles the Knatchbull family business – perhaps because of the family connection which I shall describe later. Brooke Place is now a boarding house for juniors at Ashford Independent School for Girls. Through the publicity in the *Kent Messenger* generated by my visit, I was put in touch with some other Hughes-Hallett descendants, notably Ellen Marjorie (Madge) Langsford of Ashford, who possesses an extensive Hughes-Hallett pedigree.

Frederick died on 3 April 1911, aged 85, leaving an estate valued at £52,922. He was a mason and had been appointed Grand Junior Deacon in the Grand Lodge of Mark Master Masons. Emily's mother, Jane Baggs, his first wife, was the daughter of Barnabas Baggs of All Saints' parish, Canterbury. He describes himself on his daughter's 1850 marriage certificate as 'excise officer'. I am sure that he must be the same Barnabas Baggs of Wingham who married Jane Pilcher at Littlebourne on 30 August 1820.[12] That would make them about the right age to have been the parents of Jane in 1822. Another family member is the oddly named Billinghurst Baggs, also an

CHART 9

The Hughes-Halletts

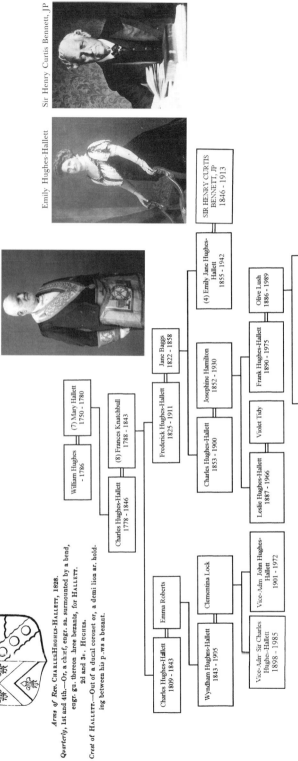

Frederick Hughes-Hallett

Emily Hughes Hallett

Sir Henry Curtis Bennett, JP

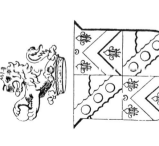

Arms of Rev. Charles Hughes-Hallett, 1828.

Quarterly, 1st and 4th.—Or, a chæf, engr. sa. surmounted by a bend, engr. gu. thereon .hree bezants, for Hallett. 2d and 3.. Hughes.

Crest of Hallett.—Out of a ducal coronet or, a demi lion ar. hold- ing between his p .ws a bezant.

William Hughes
- 1786

(7) Mary Hallett
1750 - 1780

Charles Hughes-Hallett
1778 - 1846

(8) Frances Knatchbull
1788 - 1843

Frederick Hughes-Hallett
1825 - 1911

Jane Baggs
1822 - 1858

Charles Hughes-Hallett
1853 - 1900

Josephine Hamilton
1852 - 1930

(4) Emily Jane Hughes-Hallett
1855 - 1942

SIR HENRY CURTIS BENNETT, JP
1846 - 1913

Charles Hughes-Hallett
1809 - 1843

Emma Roberts

Wyndham Hughes-Hallett
1843 - 1905

Clementina Lock

Vice-Adm. Sir Charles Hughe-Hallett
1898 - 1985

Vice-Adm John Hughes-Hallett
1901 - 1972

Leslie Hughes-Hallett
1887 - 1966

Violet Tidy

Frank Hughes-Hallett
1890 - 1975

Olive Lush
1886 - 1989

Ellen Marjorie Hughes-Hallett
1914 -

Basil Langsford Hallett
1910 - 1958

Gordon Hughes-Hallett
1917 - 1993

Sources: family papers and pedigrees; Burke's "Landed Gentry", 1952; Th Law Society; "Daily Telegraph" obituary, 6 April 1972; Berry's "Kent Genealogies", 1830; marriage certificate, 1850; "Alumni Oxonienses", 1715-1886

exciseman, 'though bred a grocer'.[13] At the time of his baptism, which took place on 4 March 1829, the family were living in Faversham. Jane died aged 36 on 6 April 1858 after giving birth to a still-born son at Barrow-hill House, Ashford. Emily was only three years old at the time. I understood from her daughter, Muriel, that she did not have a particularly happy childhood after her father married again, because she did not get on with her stepmother.

Emily's paternal grandfather, Charles Hughes (1778-1846) was yet another clergyman. Educated at Winchester and Oriel College, Oxford, he assumed the additional name of Hallett by royal licence in 1823. He had inherited property at Little Dunmow in Essex, from his uncle, James Hallett. Charles was vicar for 35 years of St Mary's, Patrixbourne, East Kent, a Norman church in a fine state of preservation. There are no less than 15 plaques to Hughes-Halletts placed one above the other inside the church, for, as the guide says, 'the family have long associations with the village'. Charles and other family members are buried together in a secluded spot in the churchyard.

The Hallett family is an old one, dating back to John Hallett who was living in Somerset at the end of the 16th century (Chart 10).[14] One of the most outstanding ancestors in this line was Sir James Hallett Kt, Lord of the Manor of Little Dunmow in Essex, a goldsmith in Cheapside and a rich man. He was Prime Warden of the Goldsmiths' Company in 1708 and was said to be the King's jeweller.[15] The son of Stephen Hallett, James was knighted in 1707. He had apparently already assumed arms which he had no right to bear, but was subsequently granted arms by the College of Arms.

Donors of the Dunmow Flitch

From 1703 for almost two hundred years Sir James and his descendants were donors of the Dunmow Flitch. In a custom originating in the 13th century in Little Dunmow, Essex, every leap year a side of bacon was presented to a couple who swore that they had not quarrelled or repented of their marriage within a year and a day of its celebration. Chaucer referred to the custom in *The Wife of Bath's Tale*. On 20 June 1751 Mary, the widow of Sir James's eldest grandson (another James) presided at a special court when the bacon was presented to a weaver, Thomas Shakeshaft and his wife Ann. They were said to have enjoyed a 'quiet, peaceable, tender and loving cohabitation'.[16] A contemporary artist, David Ogborne, illustrated the procession when the pair (known as 'pilgrims') were carried first round the churchyard and then the town in an oak chair, preceded by the bacon carried on a pole. Seven thousand people gathered to watch the spectacle and sports and music graced the day. It is recorded that afterwards Thomas and his wife cut the bacon up in slices and sold it to sightseers at a handsome profit. The custom was discontinued but revived in the mid-19th century. Since 1855, the ceremony has taken place in the town hall in Great Dunmow, two and a half miles away. The Revd. James Hughes-Hallett (1807-90) was the last family member to donate the Flitch.

CHART 10
Donor of the Dunmow Flitch

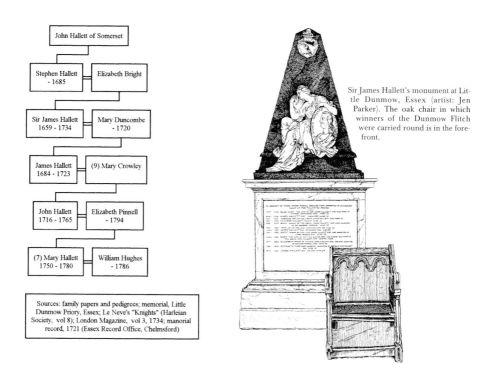

John Hallett of Somerset

Stephen Hallett - 1685 — Elizabeth Bright

Sir James Hallett 1659 - 1734 — Mary Duncombe - 1720

James Hallett 1684 - 1723 — (9) Mary Crowley

John Hallett 1716 - 1765 — Elizabeth Pinnell - 1794

(7) Mary Hallett 1750 - 1780 — William Hughes - 1786

Sources: family papers and pedigrees; memorial, Little Dunmow Priory, Essex; Le Neve's "Knights" (Harleian Society, vol 8); London Magazine, vol 3, 1734; manorial record, 1721 (Essex Record Office, Chelmsford).

Sir James Hallett's monument at Little Dunmow, Essex (artist: Jen Parker). The oak chair in which winners of the Dunmow Flitch were carried round is in the forefront.

Sir James died on 1 February 1734 at his house in Bloomsbury Square, London,[17] at that time a fashionable place in which to live. He, his wife Mary, their son James, daughter-in-law Mary (née Crowley), and great-granddaughter Mary are all commemorated in a striking obelisk on the north wall of the lady chapel at Little Dunmow, all that remains of a large Augustinian monastery, founded in the 12th century. The medallion, held by a seated female figure, bears a portrait of Sir James, who seems to be wearing a flowing wig and has a slight smile on his face. James junior, who had worked in partnership with his father at the sign of the Golden Angel, Cheapside (once the site of the chief market place of medieval London), 'ran out' of the fortune which his father settled on him. He went to France and lived there until 1723.[18]

Three Lord Mayors of London

The Hughes pedigree, too, contains people of distinction, including three Lord Mayors of London (Chart 11). Charles Hughes-Hallett's father, William Hughes, was the great-grandson of Sir John Shaw, Bart of Eltham, Kent.[19] The Shaw family was descended from Sir Edmund Shaw, Lord Mayor of London in 1382. Sir John, banker at the time of the Commonwealth, carried on business in London and Antwerp. There, he met the exiled Prince Charles (later King Charles II) and loaned him

CHART 11

The Hughes, Shaws and Peakes

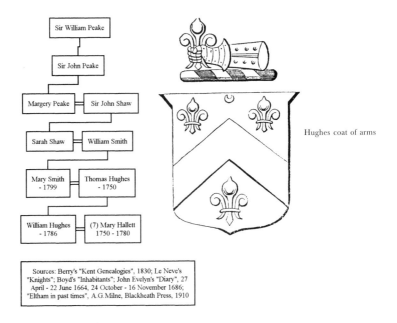

Hughes coat of arms

Sir William Peake

Sir John Peake

Margery Peake — Sir John Shaw

Sarah Shaw — William Smith

Mary Smith - 1799 — Thomas Hughes - 1750

William Hughes - 1786 — (7) Mary Hallett 1750 - 1780

Sources: Berry's "Kent Genealogies", 1830; Le Neve's "Knights"; Boyd's "Inhabitants"; John Evelyn's "Diary", 27 April - 22 June 1664, 24 October - 16 November 1686; "Eltham in past times", A.G.Milne, Blackheath Press, 1910

money. After the Restoration, Sir John was rewarded in 1665 with a baronetcy. He was trusted with so many affairs of state that Pepys recorded in his diary that he was 'a miracle of a man, holding more offices than any man in England'.[20]

Among Sir John's duties were those of surveyor of the King's woods and trustee of Queen Henrietta Maria's lands. The old palace of Eltham, ruined during the Civil War, was one of the royal estates. Its history dates back to 1086 when Odo, half-brother of William the Conqueror, held the manor of Eltham. In following centuries Edwards II and III lived there, as did Richard II. Henry IV was married by proxy to Joan of Navarre at Eltham in 1402 and it was Henry VIII's boyhood home. Sir John managed to acquire the lease of the manor of Eltham, including the palace, for himself and his heirs at a rent of £9 per annum. This included all fishing, hawking and hunting rights. He then set about rebuilding Eltham Lodge, a fine mansion which remained in the Shaw family until 1838 and later became a golf club. Sir John lived the life of a country gentleman in this house, visiting London from time to time, but not partaking in the 'wild and dissolute living' then in fashion.[21]

He was a keen churchman, and Pepys declared him to be 'a very grave and fine gentleman and good company'.[22] Sir John and his wife Margery, whom he married in 1659, are both buried in the vault beneath the old church of St John the Baptist in Eltham. Dame Margery was the daughter and sole heir of Sir John Peake, a Master of the Mercers' Company, a Sheriff and then Lord Mayor of London from 1686-87. His 'triumphant shew ... both by land and water' is mentioned in John Evelyn's diary.[23] John Peake too is buried in Eltham near his daughter. His father, Sir William

Peake, Master of the Clothworkers' Company, was also Lord Mayor from 1667-68 and it is recorded by a group of Aldermen in 1672 that he was 'diligent in the publique affaires, resolute in the King's interest and for the antient and orderly Government of the cittie'.[24]

'Snatch of the Baltic'

However, it is the wife of Charles Hughes-Hallett who provides one of the most interesting lines in the family tree. She was Frances Knatchbull, daughter of Sir Edward Knatchbull, 8th baronet, from whom the present Lord Brabourne, husband of Countess Mountbatten, is descended (Chart 12). Charles and Frances were married on 15 May 1806 at Mersham, Kent when she was just eighteen. Their ninth son, Frederick, my great-great-grandfather, was born on 28 April 1825. I first learnt of this particular family connection from my great-aunt, Muriel. In her will she left a miniature of Frances Knatchbull, wearing a lace cap with blue ribbons, to my brother David.

Burke is wrong in saying in some editions of his *Landed Gentry* that Frances was the daughter of Sir Edward by his first wife, Mary Hugessen. Sir Hughe Knatchbull-Hugessen, the diplomat and family genealogist, printed pedigrees at the end of his book *Kentish Family*[25] in which he clearly shows that Frances's mother was Frances Graham, the second wife. Sir Hughe, who *was* a descendant of the 8th baronet's first wife, Mary Hugessen, died in 1971. His nickname in the Foreign Office was 'Snatch', and he was clearly a man of some style. While Foreign Office Minister in three Baltic states between the two World Wars, he had his only secretary taken away from him. He complained by parodying the Athanasian Creed.[26] The FO, presumably impressed by Snatch's wit, immediately promoted him to be ambassador in Teheran (1934-36), then China (1936-38), followed by Ankara (1939-44).

He had his problems during this last period: his valet, an Albanian called Elyesa Bazna, turned out to be the Nazi spy Cicero. He stole secret documents from the pocket of Sir Hughe's dressing-gown and sold them to the Germans. This episode probably cost Sir Hughe his GCMG, but he went on to be ambassador to Belgium in 1944, so presumably the Foreign Office forgave him. Michael Shea refers to him in his book already mentioned, writing that Sir Hughe's name was 'one to conjure with'.[27] He quotes a number of other amusing poems Sir Hughe wrote to the Foreign Office while abroad on official duties. A friend of mine, who was entertained by Sir Hughe at his Kent home, recalls that Sir Hughe told him that he had once been briefed by Lord Curzon, that most pompous of Foreign Secretaries, while the latter was taking a bath. He was the subject of a ditty written by an undergraduate during his Oxford days. Part of it ran:

> My name is George Nathaniel Curzon.
> I am a most superior person …

My cousin Paul used to describe the Knatchbulls as 'the best family in Kent'. They have certainly made a large contribution to that county as landowners, benefactors

CHART 12

The Knatchbull connection

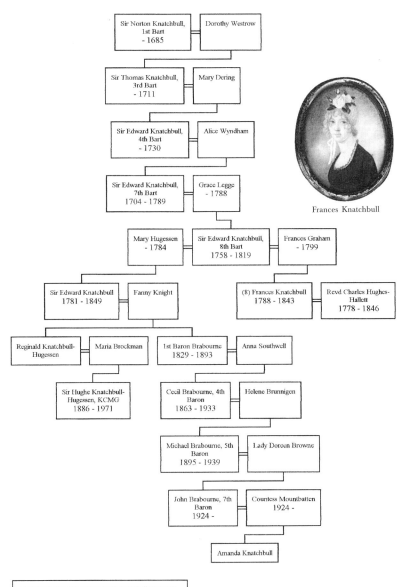

Sir Norton Knatchbull,
1st Bart
- 1685

Dorothy Westrow

Sir Thomas Knatchbull,
3rd Bart
- 1711

Mary Dering

Sir Edward Knatchbull,
4th Bart
- 1730

Alice Wyndham

Sir Edward Knatchbull,
7th Bart
1704 - 1789

Grace Legge
- 1788

Frances Knatchbull

Mary Hugessen
- 1784

Sir Edward Knatchbull,
8th Bart
1758 - 1819

Frances Graham
- 1799

Sir Edward Knatchbull
1781 - 1849

Fanny Knight

(8) Frances Knatchbull
1788 - 1843

Revd Charles Hughes-
Hallett
1778 - 1846

Reginald Knatchbull-
Hugessen

Maria Brockman

1st Baron Brabourne
1829 - 1893

Anna Southwell

Sir Hughe Knatchbull-
Hugessen, KCMG
1886 - 1971

Cecil Brabourne, 4th
Baron
1863 - 1933

Helene Brunnigen

Michael Brabourne, 5th
Baron
1895 - 1939

Lady Doreen Browne

John Brabourne, 7th
Baron
1924 -

Countess Mountbatten
1924 -

Amanda Knatchbull

Sources: "Kentish Family", Hughe Knatchbull-Hugessen,
Methuen, 1960; Burke's "Peerage"; Canterbury marriage
licences, 1781-1809; obituaries in "The Times" and "Daily
Telegraph", 6 April 1972; "Notes and Queries", April 1961

and Members of Parliament for many generations. Sir Hughe traces the family back to a Clement Nechebol who was mentioned on the Kent Assize Roll in 1278. The second Knatchbull to be knighted and the first to be made a baronet was Sir Norton Knatchbull, who represented New Romney in the Long Parliament. He died in 1685. The 4th baronet, Sir Edward Knatchbull (d.1730) was MP for Rochester and then for Kent. His namesake the 7th baronet (d.1789) was MP for Armagh, Northern Ireland. He completed Mersham Hatch (still today the seat of the Brabourne family) with the help of Robert Adam and Chippendale.

His heir Edward, the 8th baronet, caused his parents some anxiety from time to time: he ran away from his public school, got into debt at Christ Church, Oxford and generally turned out to be 'lively, impetuous and the reverse of thrifty'.[28] After the death of his first wife, Edward married Frances. Her father, John Graham, a former Deputy-Governor of Georgia, was in exile, having taken the English side during the American War of Independence. He was then living at St Lawrence, Canterbury. Frances died at the home of her father, in 1799. She had eight children in all, including a daughter, another Frances.

Within 18 months of his second wife's death Sir Edward went on to marry again. A source of much comment at the time was a huge family group portrait which he commissioned from an artist called Copley. It shows the two dead wives gazing down from the sky upon Sir Edward, his new wife and his extensive brood. Sir Edward himself is depicted holding a shotgun. He was a great hunting man, and kept a diary of his days out with the Provender Hounds. However, he too fulfilled his civic duties and was MP for Kent for two periods from 1789-1802 and from 1806-19. There is, in Sir Hughe's book, a portrait of Sir Edward by Romney. It was at one time at Parham in Sussex in the possession of the late Hon. Mrs. Clive Pearson. I am told this and other pictures now belong to Clive Gibson, a descendant of the Knatchbulls via Mary Hugessen. Sir Edward's son, the ninth baronet, married as his second wife Fanny Catherine Knight, the favourite niece of Jane Austen.

It was revealed in the national press in 1994[29] that Prince Charles proposed to his second cousin, Amanda Knatchbull, daughter of Lord and Lady Brabourne, but that she turned him down saying 'What a funny idea'. She became a social worker and married a property developer.

Slave-owner in Savannah

John Graham, father of Frances Graham and grandfather of Frances Knatchbull, was born in Scotland on 5 November 1733,[30] the son of the Revd. Alexander Pyot, a Church of Scotland minister, and Eleanor Stevenson of Whitekirk, Dunbar, East Lothian. Mr. Pyot, the son of James Pyot, a prosperous merchant of Montrose, a town councillor and elder of the church, was one of 17 children. He was educated at Marischal College, Aberdeen, started life as a schoolmaster and then entered the church. He was ordained in 1725 and became chaplain to the Marquess of Tweeddale.[31] There are different views as to the origin of the name Pyot. Horatius Bonar, a descendant, has written[32] that the family name was originally Graham. At a time when it was inadvisable to admit to belonging to the clan, one of them, when challenged, saw a magpie in the tree, and said his name was Pyot (Scottish for magpie) – and the name stuck. In any case, Alexander Pyot had John and his other children baptised with the name Graham.

Alexander seems to have been a somewhat controversial character. When he was translated to Dunbar in 1733, under the patronage of the Duke of Roxburghe, so great was the opposition to him by the congregation that on the day of the induction the church doors were locked. The minister had to break a window of the vestry to gain access. As he passed along, one of the congregation stood up and said: 'Verily, verily I say unto you, he that entereth not by the door into the sheepfold but climbeth in some other way, the same is a thief and a robber'.[33] There was also a dispute about the marriage of a soldier which resulted in a vicious satire, *Memoirs of Magopico*, written by Simon Haliburton, an army chaplain.[34]

John Graham, the eldest son, emigrated to Georgia in 1753, where he expected to inherit a relative's fortune. Evidently John was disappointed in his expectations, and so he started trading in Savannah.[35] He developed three large plantations, one of them called Mulberry Grove, 12 miles from Savannah, and accumulated 262 slaves. He was appointed to the State Council in 1763 and Deputy-Governor in 1775, a new office without salary. During the War of Independence he was taken prisoner with other members of the Council, and confined under armed guard. He escaped in an open canoe and eventually reached Boston in *HMS Scarborough*. In May 1776 he fled to England with his wife Frances and 10 children, claiming that he had left at the mercy of his enemies a fortune of £50,000 sterling. His house in Savannah and 400 barrels of rice had been burnt by 'revolutionists' who had also destroyed his vessel *Inverness* and its cargo.

Returning to Georgia in 1779, he witnessed the siege of Savannah and became superintendent of Indian affairs for the Mississippi region, with a salary of £500 per annum. When the British and the loyalists evacuated Charleston in 1782, he left for East Florida where he was given a grant of 500 acres. Eventually, for his health's sake, he sailed for England for good. Like other people loyal to the Crown who had suffered hardship, John Graham was entitled to claim compensation for his losses. His claim was heard in London and he was allowed £400 a year. In order to supplement this, he became a merchant, living for a time at 18 Queen's Row, Knightsbridge.

He died at his home at St Lawrence, Canterbury (or in Naples, Italy – accounts differ) on 11 February 1791 leaving his wife, son Charles and several daughters. John Graham's wife was Frances Crooke, a granddaughter of Robert Cunningham of South Carolina. Captain Cunningham was also an active loyalist in the American War of Independence[36] and helped assemble armed bands to support the English King in 1775.

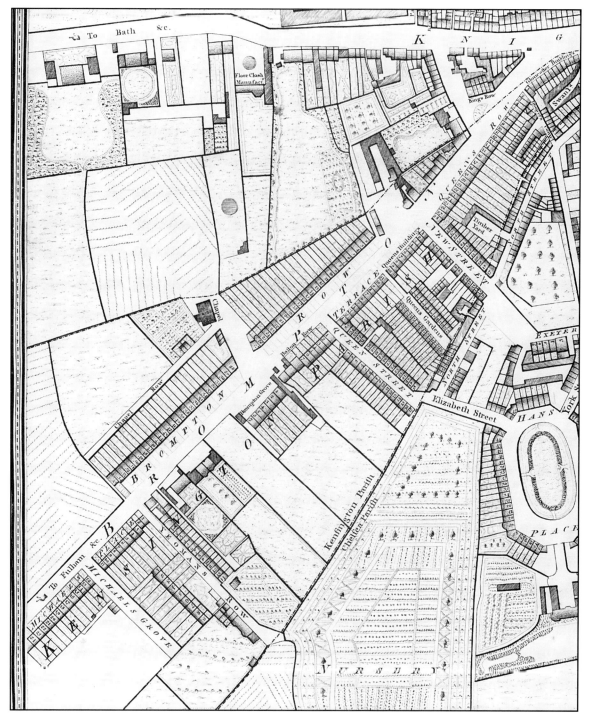

43 John Graham (*c.*1733-91) lived at 18 Queen's Row. (Photo from R. Horwood's *Map of London*, 1799, by permission of the British Library.)

How about the Honywoods?

One of my brother David's middle names is Honywood. I have often wondered about the reason for this. During the course of my research into the Hughes-Halletts and the Knatchbulls, I have found many connections with the Honywoods, who were a prominent family in both Kent and Essex. One of the 8th baronet Knatchbull's great friends and hunting companions was a Sir John Honywood, the 5th baronet. On 14 April 1834 his son, Sir John Honywood, aged 22, married Mary, aged 18, daughter of Charles Hughes-Hallett at Patrixbourne, Kent. Emily Jane Hughes-Hallett may have been specially fond of her aunt who may have replaced her dead mother. She probably wanted to commemorate the long association between the two families, for she gave the name Honywood to her eldest son, Henry Curtis-Bennett. When he was knighted, I understand that he considered calling himself 'Sir Honywood'.

Notes

[1] J. Horsfall Turner, *Ancient Bingley* (Thomas Harrison & Sons, Bingley, 1897), p.174.

[2] Stephen Foreman, *Hylands – the story of an Essex country house and its owners* (Ian Henry Publications, Romford, 1990).

[3] *Register of St Paul's Cathedral* (Harleian Society, 1889), p.133.

[4] 1851 Census.

[5] J.M. Cook (ed.), *Great Marlow: Parish and People in the 19th century* (Marten, Marlow, 1991), p.63.

[6] *London and Provincial Medical Directory* (1852).

[7] Dorking and Leith District Preservation Society newsletter no.7, Spring 1988, p.2.

[8] Dorking Tithe Apportionment Book, 1841.

[9] *Gentleman's Magazine*, new series (1852), vol.37, p.430.

[10] *Daily Telegraph*, 6 April 1972.

[11] Michael Shea, *To Lie Abroad* (Sinclair-Stevenson, 1996).

[12] *Canterbury Marriage Licences, 1810-1937* (Phillimore, Chichester, 1971), p.99.

[13] PROCUST 116/117 (PRO, Kew).

[14] B. Burke, *Landed Gentry* (1965), p.355.

[15] A.L. Reade, *Johnsonian Gleanings, Part 5* (Percy Lund Humphries, 1928), p.191.

[16] Manorial record of 1721 Award, Essex Record Office, Chelmsford.

[17] *London Magazine* (1734), vol.3, p.98.

[18] Le Neve, *Pedigree of Knights* (Harleian Society, 1873), vol.8, p.496.

[19] W. Berry, *Kent Genealogies* (Sherwood, Gilbert and Peter, 1830), p.7.

[20] R.R.C. Gregory, *The Story of Royal Eltham* (Blackheath Press, 1909), p.49.

[21] *Ibid.*

[22] *Ibid.*

[23] 29 October 1686.

[24] A.B. Beaven, *The Aldermen of the City of London* (Eden Fisher, 1913), vol.2, p.187.

[25] Sir Hughe Knatchbull-Hugessen, *Kentish Family* (Methuen, 1960).

[26] T. Braun, Dean, Merton College, Oxford, 'Snatch of the Baltic', *The Spectator*, Sept 1991.

[27] Shea, *op.cit.*, p.167.

[28] Knatchbull-Hugessen, *op.cit.*, p.138.

[29] *Daily Express*, 17 October 1994.

[30] D. Whyte, *A Dictionary of Scottish Emigrants to the USA* (Magna Carta Book Co., Baltimore, 1972), p.144.

[31] H. Scott, *Fasti Ecclesiae Scoticanae* (Oliver and Boyd, Edinburgh, 1915), vol.1, p.408.

[32] Notes to genealogical chart on pedigree of descendants of James Pyot, merchant of Montrose, Edinburgh (1914), pp.217-18.

[33] J. Miller, *History of Dunbar* (W. Miller, Dunbar, 1830), pp.217-18.

[34] Published anonymously (available British Library).

[35] *Dictionary of American Biography* (Oxford University Press, 1931), vol.7, pp.476-7.

[36] *South Carolina Historical Magazine* (South Carolina Historical Society, Charleston, 1966), vol.67, pp.15, 18-21, 23-5.

PART 5

BACK TO MEDIEVAL TIMES

Ambrose Crowley, Quaker ironmaster and patriarchal industrialist; Thomas Owen, Elizabethan Judge buried in Westminster Abbey; haunting by the White Lady of Oteley; the Blounts of Kinlet; Sara Baskerville of the House of Baskerville; Anne Ferrers, a 'gateway ancestor'; ascending to the Plantagenets and thus to Charlemagne?

Ambrose Crowley, the Quaker-born philanthropist

Emily Hughes-Hallett's ancestry has been a rich vein to explore. Apart from the Knatchbull connection, everything that I have discovered about the remoter reaches of her ancestry was previously completely unknown to me, and, I suspect, also to my father and grandfather. Emily's family tree yields perhaps the most fascinating character in this whole history: this is Sir Ambrose Crowley, whose daughter Mary in 1708 married James Hallett, Emily's great-great-great-grandfather (see Charts 10 and 13). Sir Ambrose, a self-made man *par excellence*, is rated by economic historians to be one of the most outstanding figures in the history of British industry.[1]

He was born in 1658 to a prosperous Quaker ironmonger in Stourbridge. The Birmingham area was, at that time, a stronghold of religious dissent. At the age of 16, Ambrose left the Midlands and became apprenticed to Clement Plumstead, a member of the London Drapers' Company. On arriving in the capital, Ambrose joined the Church of England, as did a number of dissenters who later became rich and amalgamated with the gentry. At an early age he showed characteristics of the enterprise and determination which marked all stages of his career. He possessed an independent and turbulent spirit, insisted on thoroughness and honesty and had a complete conviction of the correctness and validity of his principles.[2] He soon set up on his own as an iron merchant and in time his ironworks in County Durham became the largest in Europe, with customers in America and the West Indian colonies. William Penn sought his advice about establishing ironworks in Pennsylvania.

His company was a nation-wide organisation, with headquarters in Thames Street, London and later in Greenwich. There he lived in a fine 17th-century house with an interior court, a carved staircase reputed to be by Inigo Jones (who designed the nearby Queen's House) and a panelled great gallery with tall, oriel windows.

There were hints of Ambrose's trade in the little nursery which contained an iron guard to keep the children from the fire, according to the inventory of 1728.[3] The

44 Crowley House and Crowley Wharf, Greenwich, looking westwards towards the Royal Naval Hospital (from *Men of Iron*, M.W. Flinn, Edinburgh University Press, 1962).

house was pulled down in about 1855[4], but Ballast Quay, where Ambrose built a warehouse and wharf, still exists. London was the ideal centre to receive raw materials from overseas, and export finished goods to all parts of Britain and abroad. He amassed a fortune running into six figures and showed a great talent for the management of a large and complicated business.

But as remarkable as his business acumen was his philanthropy, due, perhaps, to his Quaker background. He anticipated by several generations the patriarchal industrialism of the 19th and 20th centuries. He was unique in providing a social insurance scheme including sickness, old age, unemployment and funeral benefits for workers and their children, also the services of a doctor, a minister and a schoolmaster. Ambrose was knighted 'at St James's in the bedchamber'[5] on 1 January 1707 – in the same year as his daughter Mary's father-in-law, Sir James Hallett, was knighted. Sir Ambrose also found time to be Sheriff of the City of London and in 1713 was elected MP for Andover – though he died in October of that year before he was able to take his seat in the House of Commons. The family faded out in the male line with his grandson, John. Sir Ambrose was, incidentally, granted a coat of arms.

He was immortalised by Steele in *The Tatler* as Sir Arthur de Bradly,[6] and also by Addison in *The Spectator* as Jack Anvil, alias Sir John Enville.[7] In a 'letter' to the electors of an alderman for the ward of Queen-Hithe, Steele says that Sir Arthur de Bradly (alias Crowley) tried to bribe voters with 'chaldrons of good coals gratis'. Addison also writes a satirical mock letter, this time from Crowley himself, saying that he started life as 'a person of no Extraction, with a small Parcel of rusty Iron'. Addison continues by saying that 'Jack' married Mary Owen, 'an indigent young Woman of

Quality', in order that his descendants should have 'a Dash of good blood in their Veins'. 'Jack' complains that at first his bride's father and brothers were 'exceedingly averse to this Match', but that they later dined with him almost daily, borrowing considerable sums from him. 'Our Children have been trained up from their Infancy with so many accounts of their Mother's Family, that they know the Stories of all the great Men and Women it has produced ... she thinks herself my superior in Sense as much as she is in Quality, and therefore treats me like a plain, well-meaning Man who does not know the World,' he writes plaintively.

The late Sir Anthony Wagner, onetime Garter King of Arms, notes that there is a tenuous connection with Dr. Johnson here: Sir Ambrose's half-sister, Judith, married the Revd. Cornelius Ford, a cousin of Dr. Johnson. Sir Anthony even prints a pedigree chart to show the relationship.[8] Sir Ambrose and his wife Mary Owen, whom he married in 1682 at the church of St Bartholomew the Less in London, are both buried in St Peter and St Paul, the parish church of Mitcham in Surrey. This was the parish church of Mary's family – the church at Greenwich was thought to be in too ruinous a state at the time to house so distinguished a citizen. The couple's huge, marble memorial still stands in the baptistry. The inscription to Sir Ambrose records his:

> numerous family and great estate, the present rewards of an indefatigable industry and application to business, an unblemished probity and a sincere belief and practice of true Christianity and particularly a boundless liberality towards the poor, many hundreds of whom he continually employed.

There is also reference here to the marriage of his daughter to James Hallett. The vicar at the church told me that the creator of this rather ostentatious monument was also the architect of St Martin-in-the-Fields Church in Trafalgar Square.

An Elizabethan Judge

Mary Owen's family does indeed lead to some interesting antecedents (Chart 13). The monumental inscription at Mitcham names her father as 'Charles Owen a younger son of the house of Condor'. He was the fifth son of Sir William Owen of Condover, High Sheriff of Shropshire in 1623. He in turn was the fifth son of Thomas Owen, firstly Serjeant at Law to Queen Elizabeth, then a Judge of the Common Pleas. Thomas was Recorder of Shrewsbury and the town's MP from 1584-85. He was educated at Oxford University (either at Broadgate's Hall or Christ Church) and then entered Lincoln's Inn to read law on 18 April 1562. He was called to the Bar in 1570.

He evidently took a keen interest in the affairs of the Inn, and his coat of arms is still to be seen in the Great Hall.[9] His law reports from 1583, in Latin and French, reside in a hand-written, leather volume in Gloucester Cathedral library.[10] Judge Owen died on 21 December 1598, having at the time an income of nearly £3,000 a year. He is commemorated in a splendid altar-tomb and wall-monument in Westminster Abbey, on the south aisle of the choir.[11] A life-size marble alabaster figure, clad in judicial robes and reclining on one elbow on a red and green cushion, lies between

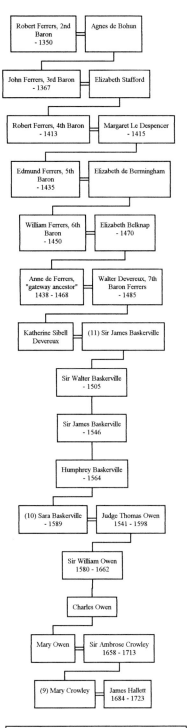

Robert Ferrers, 2nd Baron — 1350 — Agnes de Bohun

John Ferrers, 3rd Baron — 1367 — Elizabeth Stafford

Robert Ferrers, 4th Baron — 1413 — Margaret Le Despencer — 1415

Edmund Ferrers, 5th Baron — 1435 — Elizabeth de Bermingham

William Ferrers, 6th Baron — 1450 — Elizabeth Belknap — 1470

Anne de Ferrers, "gateway ancestor" 1438 - 1468 — Walter Devereux, 7th Baron Ferrers — 1485

Katherine Sibell Devereux — (11) Sir James Baskerville

Sir Walter Baskerville — 1505

Sir James Baskerville — 1546

Humphrey Baskerville — 1564

(10) Sara Baskerville — 1589 — Judge Thomas Owen 1541 - 1598

Sir William Owen 1580 - 1662

Charles Owen

Mary Owen — Sir Ambrose Crowley 1658 - 1713

(9) Mary Crowley — James Hallett 1684 - 1723

Sources: Judge Owen's monument, Westminster Abbey; Guildhall Library microfilm 2480/2; Visitations of Worcester, 1569 and Shropshire, 1623; "Genealogist's Magazine", vol 10; "Men of Iron", M.W. Flinn, Edinburgh Univy Press, 1962

CHART 13
Owens, Baskervilles and Ferrers

Sir Ambrose Crowley and his wife Mary
(from their monument in Mitcham parish church)

two Corinthian columns. He is wearing a black square hat and clutching a script. The whole memorial has been sumptuously gilded and painted, and bears a motto, given him by the Queen herself *Memorare novissima* (Remember the last things) and his own curious epitaph, *Spes, vermis et ego*[12] (Hope, worms and I).

Judge Owen built Condover Hall, an estate with 334 acres four miles south of Shrewsbury, described as the finest stone manor-house of the Elizabethan period in Shropshire.[13] A 'noted counsellor' and the only contemporary judge to be commemorated in the Abbey,[14] he designed the house himself, leaving it to his son, Roger, to complete. The house, which today is a school for the blind, is built in reddish sandstone in an 'H' shape, and the garden contains a turfed great walk and a bowling alley.

Thomas was born in the parish of St Chads, Shrewsbury, the second son of Richard Owen, a Shrewsbury solicitor. The Owen family is directly descended from Roderick the Great (or Rhodri Mawr) who was the first pre-Conquest King of all Wales.[15,16] The line of Roderick was, according to Sir Anthony Wagner, the oldest Welsh royal pedigree to have been committed to writing.[17] Roderick, the son of Merfyn the Freckled, was slain in a battle with the Saxons in 877. His wife was Angharad, daughter of Meurig, King of Greater Ceredigion. Henry VII of England was his direct descendant, as is Queen Elizabeth II.

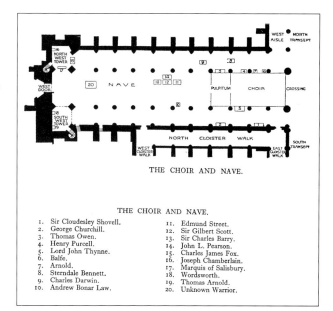

THE CHOIR AND NAVE.

1. Sir Cloudesley Shovell.	11. Edmund Street.
2. George Churchill.	12. Sir Gilbert Scott.
3. Thomas Owen.	13. Sir Charles Barry.
4. Henry Purcell.	14. John L. Pearson.
5. Lord John Thynne.	15. Charles James Fox.
6. Balfe.	16. Joseph Chamberlain.
7. Arnold.	17. Marquis of Salisbury.
8. Sterndale Bennett.	18. Wordsworth.
9. Charles Darwin.	19. Thomas Arnold.
10. Andrew Bonar Law.	20. Unknown Warrior.

45 Plan of the interior of Westminster Abbey, showing Thomas Owen's monument (no.3). (From: *Westminster Abbey and Its Ancient Art,* by J. Noppen, E. Burrows & Co., 1926.)

46 Condover Hall, Shropshire, designed by Judge Thomas Owen (from *Memories of Old Shropshire,* T. Auden, Bemrose & Sons, London, 1906).

The White Lady of Oteley

Judge Owen's mother was Mary Oteley, daughter of Thomas Oteley, an Alderman of Shrewsbury (Chart 14). In 1473 he bought Pitchford Hall, the spectacular black-and-white half-timbered Shropshire house. The north wing is thought to have been the original house, which was later enlarged and became a more elaborate E-shape building. Thomas Oteley was the third son of Philip Oteley of Oteley Hall near Ellesmere. This was formerly a Saxon nunnery given to a member of the family by the Conqueror. The inmates were expelled, and it is said that the White Lady of Oteley, the spirit of a nun, has haunted every house built by the Oteleys ever since. Thomas Oteley amassed a considerable fortune as a wool trader and was a member of the staple mart of Calais, one of the earliest organisations in English commerce, which ensured collection of Royal customs by defining channels of export.

47 Pitchford Hall (from *Memories of Old Shropshire, op.cit.*).

Mary's mother, Margaret, daughter of Sir Humphrey Blount of Kinlet, was Thomas's second wife. The Blount family is descended from Robert Le Blond of Guines, Normandy and the family name derives from their fair hair.[18] They are descended from King John through the illegitimate son of his grandson, Edmund, Earl of Cornwall. I understand from Margaret Bradley of Kidderminster, founder of the Blount One-Name study, that there is a fine effigy of Sir Humphrey and members of his family at the church of St John the Baptist at Kinlet in Shropshire. Mary's first cousin, once removed, Elizabeth Blount, a maid of honour at court, gave birth in 1519 to a son reputed to have been the child of King Henry VIII. Known as Henry Fitzroy, the child was acknowledged by the King and created Duke of Richmond and Somerset and a Knight of the Garter.[19] For a time, the King toyed with the idea of grooming Fitzroy for the throne. He was also made Lord Warden of the Marches and Lord Lieutenant of Ireland, and given a fine household, with an annuity of £4,000. There were rumours that the King was negotiating a splendid marriage for Fitzroy, with a noble or even a royal bride. Finally the King realised that it would not be feasible for a bastard to inherit the throne. In any case, Henry Fitzroy died when he was 16, 11 years before his father. [20]

CHART 14

Other possible routes to medieval times

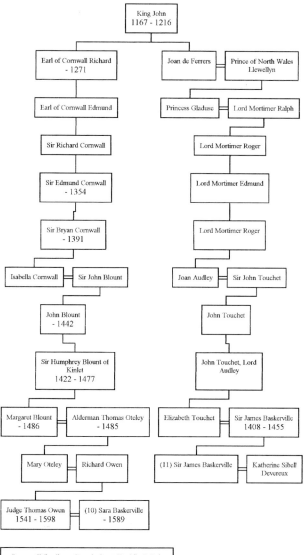

King John
1167 - 1216

Earl of Cornwall Richard
- 1271

Joan de Ferrers

Prince of North Wales
Llewellyn

Earl of Cornwall Edmund

Princess Gladuse

Lord Mortimer Ralph

Sir Richard Cornwall

Lord Mortimer Roger

Sir Edmund Cornwall
- 1354

Lord Mortimer Edmund

Sir Bryan Cornwall
- 1391

Lord Mortimer Roger

Isabella Cornwall

Sir John Blount

Joan Audley

Sir John Touchet

John Blount
- 1442

John Touchet

Sir Humphrey Blount of
Kinlet
1422 - 1477

John Touchet, Lord
Audley

Margaret Blount
- 1486

Alderman Thomas Oteley
- 1485

Elizabeth Touchet

Sir James Baskerville
1408 - 1455

Mary Oteley

Richard Owen

(11) Sir James Baskerville

Katherine Sibell
Devereux

Judge Thomas Owen
1541 - 1598

(10) Sara Baskerville
- 1589

Sources: "Miscellanea Genealogica et Heraldica", 2nd
series, vol 2; Dugdale's "Baronage of England", Tome the
First, London, 1675; "Records of an ancient family", J.E.
Ottley, Selwyn & Blount, London, 1923

*Certa Resurgendi jacet hic Sara uxor Owini
Et Baskervile femina nata Domo
Quae cum Bis septem peperisset pignora chara
Heu nimis Illa lito dum peparit periit
Digna quidem terris que plurar viveret annos
Ni fuerat sumo dignior illa Deo
Olim ac charissimae conjugi Thomas Owen
ad legem serviens posuit
obiit 12 Septems Annos Salut: 1589.*

*Arms: Arg, a lion ramp qu, a canton az:
Imp. Arg, a chev, qu, betw, three hurts.*

Sara Baskerville's
monumental inscription

After Thomas, the Oteley family continued to own the Pitchford estate for 13 successive generations, until the death of Adam Oteley without issue in 1807, when it passed into other hands. The most famous member of the family was Sir Francis Oteley, Governor of Shrewsbury during the time of Charles I. Sir Francis sheltered Prince Rupert in a priest hole during the Civil War.

Thomas died in 1485 and is buried in St Julian's Church, Shrewsbury, now a craft centre. Mourners at his funeral carried bunches of bay, rosemary and other evergreens to symbolise the soul's immortality. The service was followed by a large banquet for his friends.[21] Pitchford Hall, a Grade One mansion in which Princess Victoria (later Queen Victoria) stayed with her mother in 1835, was sold in 1992. Its unique collections of portraits, furniture, ceramics and *objets d'art* were scattered, the then owners having lost a lot of money as Lloyd's 'names'. I do not think, however, there was anything much there which went back as far as Thomas or his daughter Mary.

The House of Baskerville

The inscription on Thomas Owen's Westminster Abbey monument refers to his first wife, Sara, as 'only daughter and heir of Humphrey Baskerville'. Humphrey Baskerville was the son of Sir James Baskerville of Erdisley, Kt (d.1546)[22] (see Chart 13). Sara was baptised on 5 March 1551 in St Michael, Bassishaw, London and was buried in the same church on 12 September 1589, having had at least five sons and five daughters. This church stood in Basinghall Street near the Guildhall, but was burnt in the Great Fire in 1666. It was rebuilt but finally pulled down in 1895 and united with St Lawrence Jewry.

However, Sara's monumental inscription in St Michael's can still be seen in a bound volume[23] in the Manuscript Room at the British Library and in the Guildhall Library.[24] The inscription in Latin refers to her belonging to the house of Baskerville. This is proved by the coat of arms which goes with it (the sinister half shows the Baskerville arms – argent, a chevron gules between three hurts azure; on the dexter side are Judge Owen's arms – argent, a lion rampant and canton sable). The inscription refers to her 'twice seven' children. Dame Alice Owen, the judge's second wife, founded a boys' school in Islington, in gratitude for her escape from death in childhood, when an arrow pierced the hat she was wearing. She was also a benefactor to Emmanuel College, Cambridge, donating a fellowship and a scholarship.

Humphrey, Sara's father (the spelling of his name varies from Humfereye Baskerfeld to Baskervyle) was a mercer in the City. In the manner of many younger sons of the time, he went to London to make his fortune. He was apprenticed to one Robert Cherseye in 1541 and in due course became a freeman. Mercers were merchants who traded in all kinds of goods, especially wool and cloth. By 1559 Humphrey was Master of the Company, one of the 'Great Twelve' and the oldest livery company in the City, dating back to 1347. He was City Auditor in 1558, Sheriff from 1561-62 and Alderman from 1558-64. His parish is given in records at the Mercers' Company as that of St Michael, Basinghall Street – though he later moved to St Mary Magdalen,

Milk Street. This church was also burnt down in the Great Fire, and there is no sign of a memorial for him. He was born in Wolverley (sometimes Wolverhill), Worcestershire, as was John Baskerville, the inventor of the typeface, two centuries later. There is mention of Humphrey in a book about John's ancestry.[25] It says that Humphrey owned a meadow in Wolverley which was inherited by his son, Richard, on Humphrey's death in 1564. Richard died not long after, in 1578, and that was the end of Humphrey's branch of the family in Wolverley.

There is an interesting note in the Mercers' Company's minutes to the effect that in September 1563 Humphrey 'was one of six Aldermen who braved the plague to assist in the election of the Lord Mayor'. The minutes also record that he had the lease of a 'great house' in Milk Street.[26] It is possible that he married twice, because some pedigrees state that Humphrey Baskerville, the son of Sir James of Erdisley, married Elynor, a widow and daughter of John Aguilliam of Radnor and had two children by her. If her husband was indeed the mercer, Elynor must have died an early death, because on 5 January 1541 he married Jane Packington (or Paginton) at St Michael, Bassishaw. By her he had at least seven children, including Sara. This is confirmed in Boyd's *Inhabitants of London*.[27] Sara is also mentioned in his will, proved on 14 March 1564. It is of course possible that there were two Humphrey Baskervilles. But it is certain, however, that our Humphrey and Sara belonged to the ancient Baskerville family, because of the coat of arms. Certainly *The Visitation of Shropshire, 1623*[28] shows clear descent from Sir James Baskerville to the Humphrey who married Jane Packington.

The original Baskerville, Nicholas, came from the Norman village about ten miles south-west of Dieppe. He was a cousin of William I and his name is said to have been on the Roll at Battle Abbey, along with the names of hundreds of other families, who contributed to the building of the Abbey at Hastings. The Baskervilles were for many reigns champions to the Kings of England and were sheriffs of the county of Hereford 21 times. They were at one time obliged to present the current King with one barbed arrow every time he came to hunt in their part of the country. Erdisley Castle in Herefordshire became the Baskerville stronghold. It stood at the centre of a district where wars with the Welsh were waged with great ferocity. The castle was burnt down in the Civil War leaving only one gatehouse standing, and the family fortunes declined. Later descendants moved to Clyro Court, near Hay, in the 19th century. Sir James Baskerville (1408-55), great-great-grandfather of Humphrey, married Elisabeth Touchet, daughter of John Touchet, Lord Audley, who was Treasurer of England under Henry VII[29] (see Chart 14).

The Hound of the Baskervilles

The name Baskerville is probably associated in most people's minds with the most popular of all the Sherlock Holmes stories, *The Hound of the Baskervilles*. There is a connection: Conan Doyle, according to *Sherlock Holmes in the Midlands* by Paul Lester,[30] claims that the author was on familiar terms with the Baskervilles and borrowed their name for his story. Clyro Court is now the *Baskerville Hall Hotel*, about two miles from

Hay-on-Wye. Baskervilles are buried in the graveyard at Clyro church where the Revd. Francis Kilvert was curate when he wrote his diary. In October 1995 I visited the hotel and was told by the owner that Conan Doyle was a great walker, and during one of his stays with the Baskervilles in the late 1880s he encountered a huge dog said to have belonged to a neighbouring land-owning family, the Vaughans. They let loose the dog whenever they thought someone was trespassing on their property. Dozens of local sheep had had their throats ripped out by a huge, black beast. The Baskervilles gave Conan Doyle permission to use their name provided he did not set the scene in Wales. However, Michael Coren in *Conan Doyle*[31] gives a different account of the origins of the hound story: he claims that the author got the idea during a golfing holiday in Norfolk with a friend who told him of the old country legend. So who knows where the truth lies? While at the hotel, I saw and subsequently obtained a leaflet about the history of the family, *Baskerville Family Tree 996-1990*, revised in 1990 by Elizabeth and Peter Baskerville Rance of Sheringham, Norfolk.

Royal Connections?

When I looked more closely into the Baskerville pedigree, I found a link with not just one but several Royal families. Humphrey's great-grandfather, Sir James Baskerville, married Katherine (or Sibilla) Devereux, daughter of the 7th Baron Ferrers of Chartley.[32,33] He inherited the title through his wife Anne, daughter of the 6th Baron. Anne and her husband constitute what Sir Anthony Wagner calls 'gateway ancestors'.[34] The exceptional fertility of their progeny spread the blood royal throughout the gentry. For Anne Devereux's great-great-great-grandfather, Robert, 2nd Baron Ferrers (1309-50), married Agnes de Bohun, daughter of Humphrey de Bohun, Earl of Hereford, according to the genealogist G.E. Cockayne[35] (see Chart 13). A subsequent edition of his work[36] contests this, and names two quite different ladies as his brides.

But this Humphrey de Bohun must surely have been a member of the well-known medieval family. One of the same name married Elizabeth, daughter of Edward I in 1302. Whether this particular Humphrey was Agnes's father I have been unable to confirm absolutely. The name occurs frequently in the Bohun pedigree – I counted 11 in close succession. An article in *Family Tree Magazine*[37] by Don Steel points out that many readers must be descended from Elizabeth and Humphrey because of the fertility of their progeny. In fact, Mr. Steel asserts, 'Plantagenet descents are two a penny', whereas Tudor, Stuart, Hanoverian and Windsor descents are rare.

Edward I's line goes directly back to William the Conqueror, taking in Eleanor of Aquitaine (who claimed descent from Charlemagne, the ninth-century ruler of much of Europe, crowned Holy Roman Emperor of the West by the Pope) on the way. Eleanor's husband, Henry II, was also descended from Charlemagne through William's wife, Matilda, daughter of Baldwin, seventh Count of Flanders – and through William himself, but in the illegitimate line. Charlemagne and his Paladins are the centre of a great series of chivalric romances. He is said to have been eight feet tall, to have married nine times and to have been of such enormous strength that he could bend three horseshoes at once in his hands.

The Ferrers family is mentioned again in the history books in relation to King John, whose 'concubine' was an Agatha de Ferrers (Chart 14).[38] She gave birth to Joan, who married Llwellyn the Great, Prince of North Wales. Another line to Edward I is through his other daughter, Joan of Acre. This descent is also thanks to Katherine or Sibilla Devereux. Joan married Gilbert de Clare, Earl of Gloucester[39] and her daughter, Eleanor, married into the Le Despencer family.[40] This line also descends to Anne Devereux, her husband Baron Ferrers and their daughter Katherine.

Modern genealogists reckon that Charlemagne has no less than 20 million living descendants in today's world. Steve Jones says in his book *In the Blood: God, Genes and Destiny*[41] that we are all each other's cousins and that everybody can claim descent from William the Conqueror, usually several times over.

Notes

[1] M.W. Flinn, *Sir Ambrose Crowley Ironmonger 1658-1713*, reprinted from *Explorations in Entrepreneurial History* (1953), vol.5, no.3, p.152 (Guildhall Library, London).
[2] M.W. Flinn (ed.), *Law Book of the Crowley Ironworks* (Surtees Society, 1957), vol.167, p.xi.
[3] Flinn, *op.cit.*, p.51.
[4] *Notes and Queries* (1857), 2nd series, vol.3, p.48.
[5] Le Neve, *op.cit.*, p.495.
[6] 27 September 1709.
[7] 12 February 1712.
[8] Sir Anthony Wagner, *English Genealogy* (Phillimore, Chichester, 1983), Table 111.
[9] West window (second from left), bottom left-hand corner.
[10] MS 8.
[11] *Royal Commission on Historical Monuments (Westminster Abbey)* (HMSO, 1924), vol.1, p.57.
[12] A.R. Stanley, *Historic Memorials of Westminster Abbey* (John Murray, 1890), p.186.
[13] *Victoria County History, Shropshire* (Oxford University Press, 1968), vol.8, p.39.
[14] E.T. Murray Smith, *The Roll-call of Westminster Abbey* (John Murray, 1902), p.156.
[15] J. Burke, *History of the Commoners* (1836), vol.2, pp.509-10.
[16] *Miscellanea Genealogica Heraldica*, 2nd Series (Mitchell & Hughes, 1888), vol.2, pp.363-70.
[17] Wagner, *op.cit.*, p.29.
[18] J.E. Ottley, *Records of an Ancient Family* (Selwyn & Blount, 1923), p.43.
[19] M.M. Bradley, *Elizabeth Blount of Kinlet* (Kidderminster, 1991), p.8.
[20] Brenda Ralph-Lewis, 'The Tudors', *Family History Monthly*, November 1997, p.19.
[21] Ottley, *op.cit.*, p.52.
[22] *Miscellanea Genealogica Heraldica*, *op.cit.*, p.370.
[23] Harley 6072, f.20.
[24] GL microfilm 2480/2.
[25] Thomas Cave, *John Baskerville printer, 1706-1775, his ancestry* (G.T. Cheshire & Sons, Kidderminster, 1923), pp.7-9.
[26] Acts of Court (main minutes of the Mercers' Company).
[27] 15095/1541.
[28] *The Visitation of Shropshire, 1623* (Harleian Society, 1023), p.13.
[29] J. Hutchinson, *Herefordshire Biographies* (Jakeman & Carver, Hereford, 1890), p.9.
[30] Paul Lester, *Sherlock Holmes in the Midlands* (Brewin Books, Studley, 1992), pp.28-78.
[31] Michael Coren, *Conan Doyle* (Bloomsbury, 1995), pp.104-6.
[32] B. Burke, *Landed Gentry* (Burke's Peerage, 1952), p.125.
[33] *Visitation of Shropshire*, *op.cit.*, p.387.
[34] Wagner, *op.cit.*, p.238.
[35] G.E. Cockayne, *Complete Peerage of England, Scotland, Ireland and the United Kingdom* (G. Bell and

Sons, 1890), vol.3, p.330.

[36] Revd. V. Gibbs and H.A. Doubleday, *Complete Peerage* (St Catherine Press, 1910), vol.5, pp.311-12.

[37] January 1998, vol.14, no.3, pp.11-12.

[38] W. Dugdale, *Baronage of England* (Tome the First, 1675), p.219.

[39] C. Moor, *Manuscript Pedigrees*, book II, 517, Society of Genealogists.

[40] *Ibid.*, book I, p.162.

[41] Steve Jones, *In the Blood: God, Genes and Destiny* (HarperCollins, 1996).

PART 6

EMIGRANTS AND IMMIGRANTS

Were the Dangars Huguenots?; Henry Dangar, Australian pioneer; Albert Augustus Dangar, the 'peregrinating plutocrat'; Rouses of Rouse Hill; Baillie Mackenzie; Charles Michie, genealogist, and a possible link to Robert the Bruce; Margaret Duncan Mackintosh; the Pollocks, more clergy and lawyers; Château Latour; Conclusion

The Daring Mr. Dangar

The first wife of the second Sir Henry Curtis-Bennett was Elsie Eleanor Dangar, an heiress from Australia. They married on 4 April 1903 at St Michael's, Chester Square, London. The wedding was widely covered by the press. According to the *Essex Weekly News*, a house and a grand piano were among the wedding gifts. The bridesmaids wore red enamel brooches bearing the arms of Trinity College, Cambridge. The service was conducted by the Revd. John William Bennett, the bridegroom's uncle, and the honeymoon was spent in Biarritz. After the couple were divorced 23 years later, Elsie married an American called Henshaw, and thereafter spent her time travelling between England and Australia, spending the summer in each country. She died in 1960 and is buried in the family grave at Singleton, New South Wales.

The Dangars came from Cornwall, where family sources say they settled at the beginning of the 16th century (Chart 15). The family have always claimed to be of Huguenot origin, and this is stated in a booklet[1] commissioned by Peter Dangar of Palmerston, Armidale, New South Wales. The booklet maintains that the Dangars migrated to Jersey in the Channel Islands at the time of the Revocation of the Edict of Nantes in 1685, later moving to Cornwall, where they farmed. This claim is also made in much earlier printed material.[2]

Elisabeth Mary Dangar, a great-granddaughter of Henry Dangar 'The Pioneer', who was one of the first to colonise New South Wales, has also produced a booklet on the family.[3] In this she appears to demolish the Huguenot theory calling it the 'Huguenot myth'. She claims it has been disproved by her cousin, Dudley Frederick Oliphant Dangar (Freddy) of Dittisham, South Devon. He did a great deal of research among Cornish records, and traced the family back to a Nicholas Dangar of Tretheven who married Joanna Pawlye on 28 November 1579. This was 106 years before the Revocation of the Edict of Nantes in 1685. Nevertheless, Huguenots did start leaving France after the Massacre of St Bartholomew, ordered by the French King Charles IX in 1572. Migrations to England and other countries by Huguenots are well documented to have taken place even earlier, in the 1560s, including to the Channel Islands. Jersey could have been a convenient stepping-stone on the way to England.

The first French church at Southampton which was established as early as during the reign of Edward VI (1537-53) was largely fed by refugees from the Channel Islands.[4] Not many Huguenots went to the West Country or became farmers, but some undoubtedly did.

Nicholas was the first recorded Dangar of this branch, but the date and place of his birth are not known. He died in 1599 and is buried, like his wife, children and grandchildren, at St Kew, Cornwall. Freddy Dangar found records of many Dangars living near Bodmin Moor in the 16th and 17th centuries, with the name sometimes being spelt Danguerd, Dangerd and Danger. Dangars was certainly a Huguenot name. *The Proceedings of the Huguenot Society*[5] mentions two members of the Huguenot clergy – Guillaume Gustave Daugars (or Dangars) and W.D. Dungars (or Dangars) who were both associated with the French church in Threadneedle Street, London in the mid-19th century. The Huguenot Library at University College, London also has many records of names similar to Dangar – which, after all, is not a typically English name. There are people called Dangé, Dangeau, Dangier and Dangre among their records. Presumably all these people anglicised their names as they settled in England.

Henry Dangar, the son of William, was born on 18 November 1796 at Lampen Farm in the parish of St Neot. Henry was baptised in the local church at St Neot on 25 January 1797. His mother was Judith, daughter of John Hooper of Bodmin. We do not have many details about Henry's early life, except for a phrase he used in a letter in which he states he 'was bred a surveyor'.[6] The first positive information we have is that a family friend brought Henry to the notice of the first Earl of St Germans, who recommended that Henry be allowed to emigrate to New South Wales. This was necessary at this time, for New South Wales was still looked upon as a convict colony. Henry arrived in Sydney on 2 April 1821, and he soon succeeded in making his mark. On 1 July of the same year he was appointed Assistant Surveyor by the Governor. He was told to survey the Hunter river valley, with a view to making land available to settlers. He also laid out a plan for the township of Newcastle. However, in 1827 he became involved in a dispute which resulted in his dismissal from office.

He was accused of improperly appropriating land near Scone to himself and his brother, William. He returned to England to protest against the Governor's accusation. On the voyage he prepared a book called *The Emigrant's Guide* containing maps, an index and directory to the Hunter river and surrounding countryside. This book is now in the Mitchell Library in Sydney. While in England he married Grace Sibley, also from St Neot, on 13 May 1828. Then he joined the Australian Agricultural Company, with whom he had already come into contact in Australia. He returned there with his bride in 1829, and in 1832 they settled at Neotsfield near Singleton. Henry had a grant of land dating from his Government appointment, and turned his attention more and more to animal husbandry. He soon became one of the new colony's most successful pastoralists, a member of the 'squattocracy', with vast land

CHART 15
The Daring Dangars

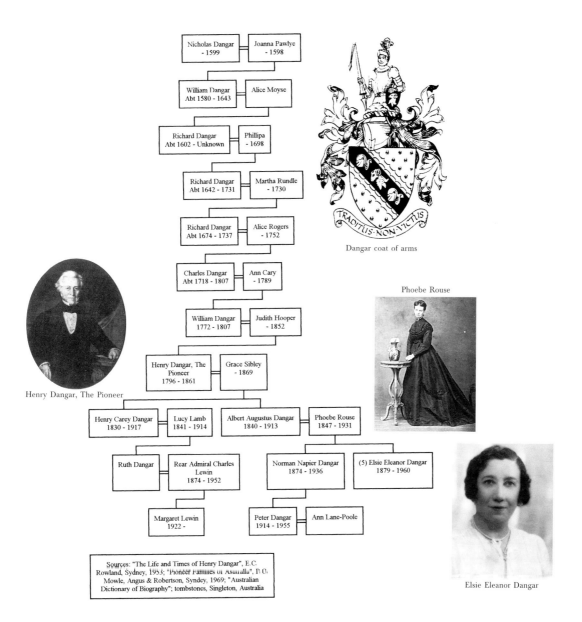

Dangar coat of arms

Henry Dangar, The Pioneer

Phoebe Rouse

Nicholas Dangar
- 1599

Joanna Pawlye
- 1598

William Dangar
Abt 1580 - 1643

Alice Moyse

Richard Dangar
Abt 1602 - Unknown

Phillipa
- 1698

Richard Dangar
Abt 1642 - 1731

Martha Rundle
- 1730

Richard Dangar
Abt 1674 - 1737

Alice Rogers
- 1752

Charles Dangar
Abt 1718 - 1807

Ann Cary
- 1789

William Dangar
1772 - 1807

Judith Hooper
- 1852

Henry Dangar, The Pioneer
1796 - 1861

Grace Sibley
- 1869

Henry Carey Dangar
1830 - 1917

Lucy Lamb
1841 - 1914

Albert Augustus Dangar
1840 - 1913

Phoebe Rouse
1847 - 1931

Ruth Dangar

Rear Admiral Charles Lewin
1874 - 1952

Norman Napier Dangar
1874 - 1936

(5) Elsie Eleanor Dangar
1879 - 1960

Margaret Lewin
1922 -

Peter Dangar
1914 - 1955

Ann Lane-Poole

Elsie Eleanor Dangar

Sources: "The Life and Times of Henry Dangar", E.C.
Rowland, Sydney, 1953; "Pioneer Families of Australia", D.O.
Mowle, Angus & Robertson, Syndey, 1969; "Australian
Dictionary of Biography"; tombstones, Singleton, Australia

48 & 49   From the Dangar farm, St Neot, Cornwall ...to Neotsfield, Singleton, New South Wales

holdings. He was also an important public figure, serving as a magistrate and a member of the Legislative Council for Northumberland from 1845 until 1861, the year of his death.

On 3 October 1854 the Dangar family was granted a coat of arms and chose as their motto *Traditus non Victus* (Yielded not Conquered). The choice of this phrase refers to the family's conviction that they were of Huguenot stock. Henry succeeded in bringing his six brothers and one sister with him to Australia, and there are very few Dangars left in Cornwall today. Elsie's father Albert Augustus (known as Abby) was born in 1840, the fourth son of Henry and Grace. Abby spent three years of his boyhood at sea. Then he too became a successful pastoralist, specialising in the breeding of Suffolk Punch horses, Merino sheep, long-woolled Devons and Shorthorn cattle at the family estate at Gostwyck station near Armidale.

Rouse of Rouse Hill

Abby married Phoebe, daughter of Edwin Rouse of Rouse Hill and Hannah Hipkins. Edwin and Hannah were married on 24 September 1840 at St James's Church in Sydney. Hannah had newly arrived from England, and had probably gone to Australia with her aunt, her own mother having died when she was thirteen. Edwin had been very impressed the first time he saw her because she was busy in the kitchen making damper (an Australian form of unleavened bread).

Hannah was baptised on 6 August 1820 at Tipton in Staffordshire, the daughter of Stephen Hipkins and Nancy Baker. Stephen described himself variously as a blacksmith, a nail factor and an ironmonger. The family lived in the Midlands long before the Industrial Revolution and had been mainly skilled artisans and tradesmen. It is said that Hannah was well educated and used to read Dickens and Scott to her grandchildren. She was also interested in music and her letters reveal that she was very religious.

The Rouse family has been researched by Caroline Thornton of Perth, also a descendant.[7] She has discovered that the family originated in Oxford, England, and that Edwin's grandfather, Richard Rouse, had been a successful cabinet maker, but had gone bankrupt after dabbling in china dealing. Their son, also Richard, born in 1774 in the Jericho part of the city (then outside the city walls) was only seven when this happened. He married Elizabeth Adams, daughter of an Oxford victualler, in 1796, and on 30 April 1801 they set sail for Australia with their family aboard the *Nile.* They landed at Sydney Cove on 14 December in the same year. As a free settler, Richard was entitled to a grant of land, seed for crops and food for the first year of settlement. To begin with, the family lived in a tent, then in a marquee in the area which later became Sydney cricket ground.

50   Albert Augustus Dangar's splendid home, Baroona, Singleton, New South Wales.

In time Richard became prosperous, largely through his cattle breeding and horse stud businesses. By 1846, six years before his death, he owned 1,200 acres. The grant of 450 acres at Rouse Hill, north of Sydney, had officially been given him in 1816, although he had assumed possession of the land three years earlier. Edwin, Richard and Hannah's third son and Phoebe's father, became the second owner of Rouse Hill. Today Rouse Hill House still stands as Australia's oldest large family house, used by six generations of the Rouse family. It was visited in 1971 by John Betjeman, the British writer and Poet Laureate, who featured it in a BBC TV programme about early Australian houses. In 1987 the house became the responsibility of the Historic Houses Trust.

Abby Dangar, Phoebe's husband, was also a large landowner in the city area of Newcastle. They lived in a splendid house called Baroona, at Singleton, which also

51   The Dangar mausoleum at All Saints', Singleton, New South Wales

stands to this day. Known as a 'peregrinating plutocrat',[8] he was generous to Singleton, where he donated a cottage hospital. Perhaps in memory of his days at sea, in 1909 he gave £10,000 to a fund providing a Dreadnought battleship as a gift to Britain from Australia. His probate after his death in 1913 was sworn at £300,000.

Henry and his wife Grace are also buried in the impressive family mausoleum in the graveyard of All Saints' Church at Singleton, New South Wales. Abby was the benefactor of this church and his wife laid the foundation stone in 1875.

North of the Border

Now at last we come to the heritage of my mother, Margaret Duncan Mackintosh (always known as Margot) (Chart 16). She was born on 4 May 1904 at Camden Cottage, between the post office and the police station in Aboyne, Aberdeenshire. Her parents were Dr. Duncan Mackintosh and his wife, Elizabeth Mackenzie. Aboyne, 'place of rippling waters', was recognised as a burgh by Royal Charter in 1676. Margot was baptised in the nearby 'Wee Free' church. Her ancestry is entirely Scottish. Some years ago she gave me a family tree tracing her maternal ancestors, via the Mackenzie, Michie, Forbes and Hay families, back to Robert the Bruce (1274-1329), the Scottish king. She copied this tree from one belonging to her uncle, Dr. John Mackenzie, a graduate of Aberdeen University.[9]

52 & 53 Margot Mackintosh as a 16-year-old ... and on her return from Paris

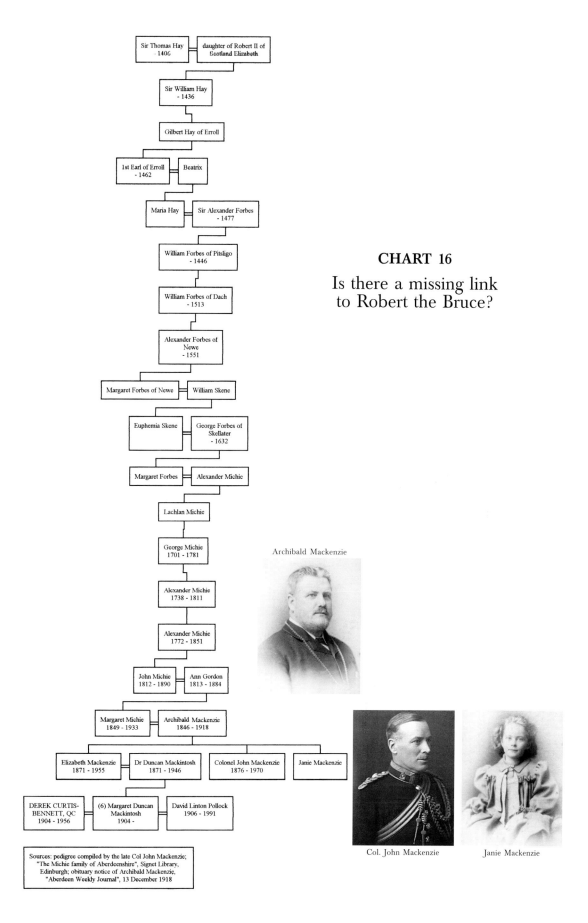

Sir Thomas Hay
- 1406

daughter of Robert II of
Scotland Elizabeth

Sir William Hay
- 1436

Gilbert Hay of Erroll

1st Earl of Erroll
- 1462

Beatrix

Maria Hay

Sir Alexander Forbes
- 1477

William Forbes of Pitsligo
- 1446

William Forbes of Dach
- 1513

Alexander Forbes of
Newe
- 1551

Margaret Forbes of Newe

William Skene

Euphemia Skene

George Forbes of
Skellater
- 1632

Margaret Forbes

Alexander Michie

Lachlan Michie

George Michie
1701 - 1781

Alexander Michie
1738 - 1811

Alexander Michie
1772 - 1851

John Michie
1812 - 1890

Ann Gordon
1813 - 1884

Margaret Michie
1849 - 1933

Archibald Mackenzie
1846 - 1918

Elizabeth Mackenzie
1871 - 1955

Dr Duncan Mackintosh
1871 - 1946

Colonel John Mackenzie
1876 - 1970

Janie Mackenzie

DEREK CURTIS-
BENNETT, QC
1904 - 1956

(6) Margaret Duncan
Mackintosh
1904 -

David Linton Pollock
1906 - 1991

CHART 16

Is there a missing link
to Robert the Bruce?

Archibald Mackenzie

Col. John Mackenzie

Janie Mackenzie

Sources: pedigree compiled by the late Col John Mackenzie;
"The Michie family of Aberdeenshire", Signet Library,
Edinburgh; obituary notice of Archibald Mackenzie,
"Aberdeen Weekly Journal", 13 December 1918

He joined the Royal Army Medical Corps in 1902, having won the Marshall Webb prize for gaining the highest marks in medical military administration on the passing-out course. Half his army service was spent in India, where he became honorary surgeon to the Viceroy. He retired from the RAMC in 1941 with the rank of Colonel, and died in Worthing in 1970, aged ninety-four. He was a vigorous man who once skated along the frozen river Dee from Aboyne to Aberdeen, a distance of about 30 miles, and enjoyed sea-bathing off the Sussex coast. Kenneth, his son, also a doctor, told me that his father spent many years tracing records and visiting burial grounds, searching for the ancestors of his mother, Margaret Michie. According to Kenneth, Uncle Jack, as we called him, was able to prove the ascent back to the Bruce except for one missing link. This was confirmed by my grandmother, Elizabeth, who told Margot that there was one marriage which could not be proved. Unfortunately, apart from the pedigree chart, none of Uncle Jack's papers survives. Margot told me that the research was done by Charles Michie, the second cousin of her maternal grandmother. Charles Michie, born on 14 May 1869, was the son of the University Librarian at Marischal College, Aberdeen.

Charles was educated at Silver Street Academy and the Grammar School, Aberdeen. He also spent much of his working life in India working in the jute industry. Nevertheless he undertook extensive research into the Michie family, probably in his retirement, and records of this are scattered in various Scottish libraries. The name Michie is an Aberdeenshire surname derived from Michael, and Michies

54 & 55   Margaret Michie (1849-1933) in youth … and old age

are a sept of the Macdonald clan. When Charles Michie died in June 1923, his passing was noted by *Scottish Notes and Queries*[10] saying that he had 'a keen and discriminating taste for genealogy and accumulated a vast amount of data connected with northern Scottish families'. This publication, to which he had been a 'prominent subscriber', noted that he had been awarded a CBE for efficient service to government in connection with war pensions and disablement relief departments.

I think that the truth of the matter is that Charles Michie researched his own paternal family, and Uncle Jack tried to make the link with the Bruce. I have checked the pedigree drawn up by the latter. Despite searching the old parish records in Aberdeen, I have not yet found evidence of the existence of Alexander Michie who married Margaret Forbes, the parents of Lachlan Michie. This must be the missing link to which Kenneth Mackenzie referred. Everything else on the chart seems to be correct. The link with the Forbes family, ascending to Sir John Forbes 'with the black lip' and beyond,[11] also depends on proving that the Margaret Forbes who married Alexander Michie was the daughter of George Forbes of Skellater. The Michies, Forbes and Skenes were all Aberdeenshire families, so intermarriage between them would seem to be natural.

Peter Drummond-Murray of Mastrick, Slains Pursuivant of Arms, attached to the Court of the Lord Lyon King of Arms in Edinburgh, has done a great deal of research into the Michies because his daughter married into the family. He told me that Charles Michie's work was appallingly presented but seemed to be accurate. He kindly sent me some of his papers referring to the Michies. They show that Margaret, daughter of George Forbes of Skellater, married Robert, not Alexander, Michie of Lochans. Dr. Toby Carter of Crewkerne, Somerset, a descendant of James Michie of Strathdon, also confirms this marriage; but, he writes to me, there was a great number of Michies at or near Strathdon, many of them called Alexander or Robert. There was also a great number of Forbeses. Dr. Carter has a note of Lachlan Michie alive in 1687, but no information about whether or whom he married. So we must conclude that our Michie link to Robert the Bruce is still possible, but not yet authenticated.

More information about Robert the Bruce has come to light in recent years. He died of leprosy in 1329, and was buried in Dunfermline Abbey – without his heart. It was his dying wish that his heart be cut out and taken to the Holy Land by his friend, Sir James Douglas. He was known as Black Douglas to the English and played a key role at the battle of Bannockburn in 1314. However Bruce's heart never made it there. Legend has it that it got only as far as Spain, carried by Douglas in a lead, cone-shaped casket and was brandished to inspire the Crusaders fighting the Moors. It is said that during one battle Douglas found himself surrounded, hurled the casket into the fray and dived in after it to his death. The casket was found on the battlefield and returned to Scotland to be buried at Melrose Abbey, 60 miles from where the Bruce's body lies, in Dunfermline Abbey. In 1996[12] archaeologists dug up a lead container from a shallow trench which they believed held the mummified heart. After carbon dating of the casket, which confirmed it was from around 1300, the heart was re-buried at Melrose in June 1998.

The Times reported earlier in 1996[13] that it was really Douglas who saw the struggles of the spider, not the king. Sir Walter Scott is thought to have perpetuated the legend of Bruce while in hiding being so encouraged by a spider's perseverance that he resolved to try and try again.

Baillie Mackenzie

My Mackenzie grandmother's father and husband of Margaret Michie was Archibald Mackenzie, a member of the second largest clan in Scotland. Archibald, according to his marriage certificate, started out as a clerk to a coal merchant. Later he founded *The Aberdeen Trawl Owners and Traders Engineering Company*. He owned a fleet of ships which used to carry coal from Scotland to the south of England. When he died in 1918 he left shares in his company to all members of his family, and Margot eventually inherited some of these. She also inherited some of the feu duties he owned in Cults, near Aberdeen. One of the executors of his lengthy will was his wife's cousin, Charles Michie.

Archibald was obviously a person of some prosperity and a person of consequence in the locality – he was a JP for Aberdeenshire. One of my Scottish relatives told me that he was offered a knighthood, but refused it. His obituary in the *Aberdeen Weekly Journal* in 1918[14] described 'Baillie Mackenzie' as 'a keen businessman and a

56 1870 marriage certificate of Archibald Mackenzie and Margaret Michie (reproduced with the kind permission of the Registrar General for Scotland).

ready speaker who was one of the most useful members of the boards on which he served'. These included the Aberdeen Town Council, then the City Parish Council and District Lunacy Board. He is also described as having been 'conspicuously successful' as a police magistrate.

Margot remembers spending much time with him in her Scottish childhood at his home, Dunmail, Cults and indeed claims that he spoilt her as the eldest grandchild. She recalls driving to the Braemar Games with him in one of the first motor cars seen in the district. She also remembers waiting at the bottom of his garden to wave to King Edward VII as he passed by in his white train on his way to Balmoral. An only child, Margot was generally indulged by her Mackenzie relatives. One aunt sent her a grey squirrel

57   The Mackenzie home at Dunmail, Cults, Aberdeenshire.

coat from China. She used to have a new hat each Easter and particularly remembers one in red straw, decorated with cherries. Her grandfather was a kind man who used to pick the best flowers in the greenhouse to present to the conductresses on the trams which took him from Cults to Aberdeen and back again. His wife was not always very pleased about this.

My maternal grandfather, Duncan Davidson Mackintosh, trained as a doctor at Marischal College, Aberdeen University,[15] graduating in 1892 with honourable distinction. He was determined to marry my grandmother and used to wait for her outside her school in Crown Street where the Mackenzie family lived before they moved to Cults. They married on 6 October 1897 at Cults Free Church, one of the last bastions of Puritanism and Sabbatarianism, and honeymooned in Montrose. Duncan practised medicine in Aboyne, and in those days used to ride a motorbike. He would visit his patients in all weathers, speaking Gaelic to them, if necessary. After working at the Red Cross Auxiliary Hospital in Aboyne from 1914-15, he wanted to contribute more to the war effort. He and his family moved to London, where he worked as a civil surgeon tending war wounded at the First London General Hospital, south-east London, from 1916-18.

After WW1 a distinguished London surgeon, Sir d'Arcy Power, wanted Duncan to go into partnership with him. But Duncan preferred to live in the country and moved with his family to Worthing on the south coast. They were eventually joined there by other Mackintosh and Mackenzie relatives, including Margaret Michie. Duncan built up a family practice there, was elected President of the Sussex branch of the British Medical Association in 1936, and was a President of the Brighton, Hove

58 Duncan Mackintosh (1871-1946) and his wife Elizabeth at home in Worthing, Sussex.

and District Caledonian Society. He was a freemason and a past master of the Beckett lodge. He died in 1946 and his widow in 1955. Both were cremated at Worthing cemetery.

Duncan's parents were William Mackintosh, an insurance agent, and Mary Symon. They were married in Aberdeen on 15 October 1864. The certificate from the Edinburgh Register Office shows William to have been a widower at the time of the wedding, and the son of Duncan Mackintosh, a farmer. Mary was the daughter of John Symon, a furniture dealer who lived at Glenburnie House, West Aberdeen but whose premises were at 29 Upperkirkgate. His wife was Elizabeth Taylor. Duncan must have acquired his love of antiques, which he collected, from his maternal grandfather. He also made furniture as a hobby from locally felled oak.

Speaking of her Mackintosh relatives, I have heard Margot say that one of her father's cousins, Hugh Mackintosh, was Moderator of the General Assembly of the Church of Scotland. On the Mackenzie side, one of her most attractive aunts was Janie Mackenzie, Jack's sister. She graduated in modern languages at the University of Aberdeen in 1909.[16] During WW1 she joined the Voluntary Aid Detachment (VAD) and did other voluntary work in Aberdeen from 1914-15. Then she worked in the Intelligence Service in Alexandria and in the Ministry of Finance, War Department in Cairo from 1916-18,[17] mainly in the censorship department. When her younger sister, Chris, got married, Janie had to give up her job with the League of Nations in Paris and return home to act as a companion to her widowed mother.

Glimpsed at a May Ball

Margot moved to England with her parents during WW1 at the age of twelve. She remembers seeing the Fleet lit up as the train passed over the Forth Bridge, and experiencing great excitement at visiting England for the first time. She and her mother lived at first in Bloomsbury where Duncan was working in a hospital for officers, and then in a hotel in Champion Hill, near the hospital to which Duncan had then moved. She remembers being taken round the wards to cheer the patients up, and also seeing a Zeppelin on fire. Margot, who had been taught by governesses in Scotland, was sent to a boarding school in Sutton, Surrey. She very much disliked this, as she was teased for her Scottish accent and because she had a boy's middle name. She recalls that her classmates offered to pay her twopence if she would recite a verse of Burns' poetry – and give them all a good laugh.

When the family moved to the south coast four years later, she was sent to a local day school, St Michael's, Hove. Next door was the home of Mr. Colman of mustard fame, all of whose windows were painted yellow. Margot took her School Certificate in the *Old Ship Hotel* in Brighton which can trace its history back to 1559. It was once the site of royal gatherings and society balls – George IV, Paganini, Thackeray and Dickens all stayed there.

Later her mother, who had been educated in Dresden and Lausanne, sent her to stay with a family in Paris for two years, despite the objections of her father, who never went abroad at all during his whole life, despite the proximity of the Channel. So keen was my grandmother that her daughter should acquire the right French accent that she hired an actor from the Comédie Française to coach her once a week. The family took her to a French wedding, where she was greatly impressed by the elaborateness of the clothes and the food. This exposure to French culture was invaluable when she worked at General de Gaulle's headquarters at Carlton Gardens in WW2. She relates that she often spoke to the great man himself (who would speak only French). She once slipped on a greasy patch on the floor when taking him his lunch, and awoke to find herself in the basement medical centre. I remember her saying that, after the divorce from Derek, she was offered a job in MI6 by Sir Dick White, head of foreign security, because of her good French.

When she returned to England after her sojourn abroad, Margot was rather frustrated when her father stipulated that when she went to dances she must return by midnight. So, like Cinderella, she had to leave the ball when it was at its height to find him sitting up waiting for her to return. He would not speak to her for two weeks after she had her hair shingled, as was fashionable in the '20s. A great influence on her in Worthing was the family of 'Tiger' Jackson, a Calcutta lawyer who returned to England to see his family each summer. Yolande, the daughter, was at school with Margot, and I believe later married a Russian Prince she met on the French Riviera. Her brother, nicknamed Joe (later Sir Richard Jackson, Assistant Commissioner of the CID at Scotland Yard and President of INTERPOL) was at Cambridge with Derek. After Margot completed her school education, she took a secretarial course in St James's Street, London, and then moved into the Jackson home as secretary to Mrs. Jackson. Her father did not altogether approve, finding the family rather 'fast'.

Margot first noticed Derek at a May Ball at Trinity College, Cambridge, and says she was later introduced to him by a mutual friend at the *Savoy Hotel*. They were engaged for two years before they got married, so that Derek could establish himself at the Bar. The banns were called in Worthing and also in St James's, Piccadilly, as my grandfather was then living in Half Moon Street. The young couple finally married in Worthing on 21 July 1928. Local newspapers reported that Heene parish church was so full for the ceremony that many people had to stand in the porch. There were four bridesmaids dressed in pink taffeta and chiffon, with bouquets of red

59 & **60** Wedding of Derek Curtis-Bennett and Margot Mackintosh in Worthing; the Very Revd. Owen Dampier-Bennett, the Dean of Nassau (1874-1950), is on the right. And *(left)* the Curtis-Bennetts at somebody else's wedding.

roses. Emily Curtis-Bennett, the groom's grandmother, also carried a bouquet of shaded sweet peas – this was the fashion at the time. The reception was held at the Mackintosh home, St Elmo, Victoria Road, Worthing, where the many wedding presents were displayed and an orchestra played a selection of Scottish airs. The honeymoon was spent in Aix-les-Bains and Annecy.

More clergy and lawyers – the Pollocks

We three children had a very happy childhood, spent mostly in London when we were not at boarding school. Margot – who had always secretly hankered after having a career of her own – became very involved in voluntary work for the London Police Court Mission (later the Rayner Foundation), to which she had been introduced by her grandmother-in-law, Emily Curtis-Bennett. Margot sat on a number of committees concerned with providing hostels for probation officers and running approved schools for young offenders, and displayed a natural talent for organisation. A woman of great detemination, she was described jokingly by Derek: 'Margot wasn't born in Aberdeen, she was carved out of the granite'.

We were very sad when our parents' marriage broke up. After my parents were divorced in 1949 Margot married David Linton Pollock, who also came from a family of churchmen and lawyers. They descend from a David Pollock, saddler to George III, and David's wife Homera. This pair had three remarkable sons, a Chief Justice of Bombay (my stepfather's great-grandfather), a Lord Chief Baron and a Field Marshal. The saddler's father was a Burgess of Berwick-on-Tweed, and the family claims descent from Fulbert de Pollock, who arrived in Scotland from France in the 11th century. His ancestor was probably Clovis, King of the Franks.[18]

David Pollock's father, the Revd. Charles Pollock (1858-1944), was a Fellow and Bursar of Corpus Christi College, Cambridge and sixth Wrangler – in other words, he was the sixth most successful performer in the Mathematical Tripos. He was made an honorary freeman of the borough of Cambridge in recognition of his services as a councillor and alderman for 50 years. A collateral, Viscount Hanworth, was Master of the Rolls from 1923 to 1935 and a plaster profile of him used to hang in one of the ground floor rest rooms in the old Public Record Office in Chancery Lane. A grandson of the saddler, Baron Charles Edward Pollock of the Exchequer (1823-1897), was chairman of the committee which built my local church, All Saints', Putney Lower Common – a Grade II listed building – in 1874.

His nephew, Sir Frederick Pollock, Bart., conducted a spirited correspondence for nearly 50 years with Oliver Wendell Holmes, Justice of the Supreme Court of the United States. This was published by the Cambridge University Press in 1942. Grace Pollock (née Blenkin), Charles' wife, was related to the Trollope family. She claimed to trace her ancestry back to Hotspur (Henry Percy) and thence to Edward III, great-grandfather of Hotspur's wife, Elizabeth. Her granddaughter, Mary Crossley, sent me a pedigree showing these ascents.

David Pollock, like Derek, was a Trinity man. Many members of the Pollock family have been undergraduates at that college – 60 at the last count. David was a partner in the firm of Freshfields, solicitors to the Bank of England. According to *Freshfields 1743-1993*,[19] he became a partner in the firm in 1931. He was called to the Treasury in 1939 to help draft the first Exchange Control regulations. He then left for active service in WW2, serving with distinction as a Commander in the Royal Naval Volunteer Reserve (RNVR) and playing a prominent part in the Royal Navy's defence communications in the Pacific. After the war he was a member of the British Government's economic mission to Argentina in 1946. As the youngest – and best-looking – member of the delegation, he was detailed to dance with Eva Peron. Unfortunately I could never extract from him any details of their conversation. The following year, he acted as adviser on the sale of the British-owned Argentine Railways.

Soon after he married Margot in 1950, David joined Pearson plc as head of the legal department, and became a member of the board. He and Lord Poole were credited, at an address given by Lord Gibson at Lord Cowdray's memorial service in 1995, with having helped to reshape the Pearson group in the post-war world. One of David's assignments was to organise the selling of the Athens-Pireas Electricity Company to the Greek Government. As he was President of this company, he enjoyed the pleasure of being able suddenly to floodlight the Parthenon at the end of a dinner party he gave for the President of Greece in the Grande Bretagne hotel. David was also a director of the National Westminster Bank, Vickers Ltd. and the Legal and General Assurance Society.

61   David and Margot Pollock meet King Paul of Greece in Athens in 1960.

Perhaps the apex of his career was to become for 15 years President of Château Latour, which was owned by Pearson's at that time. Here he boldly introduced, against the conventional wisdom of the day, the use of stainless steel vats. This caused a sensation among the French, who accused him of turning Latour into a milk parlour. But many other châteaux have since copied his example. Margot and he had the château decorated by the fashionable John Fowler with 'Sussex charm and comfort', as one French magazine put it. In June 1974 they entertained the Duke of Edinburgh who stayed overnight in the château. His bodyguard slept in the hall and the Duke was followed by an ambulance carrying blood of his group. The Queen Mother and the Prince of Wales also visited Latour during David's presidency. Margot and David met the Duke and Duchess of Windsor at a dinner party at Château Mouton given

62   Château Latour, near Bordeaux, where
David Pollock was president for 15 years.

63   David Pollock (left) with Prince Philip when
he became a member of the Académie du Vin
de Bordeaux in 1976.

by Baron Philippe de Rothschild. They found the Duchess 'very quiet', rather contrary to their expectations.

David and Margot rebuilt the Old Rectory at Wiggonholt in West Sussex. The house stands on a hill with a lovely view over the Arun wild brooks and the South Downs. It was conveniently near Itchenor where David was at one time Rear-Admiral of the sailing club. He was also a member of the Royal Yacht Squadron at Cowes, Isle of Wight and is said to be the only person ever known to resign from that prestigious membership, as he did on his retirement. We spent many happy holidays and weekends at Wiggonholt, a place of supreme comfort, of log fires and linen sheets.

David suffered from painful back trouble in his final years, and died in September 1991. He is buried in the churchyard at Wiggonholt where he was churchwarden from 1961-81. Lord Blakenham, Chairman of Pearson's, gave the address at his funeral, which was attended by Lord Cowdray, the company's president. David presented the hassocks to the church, as well as the prie-dieu which stands by the altar and was carved by his remarkable mother who was a considerable artist.

His gravestone was designed John Skelton, a Sussex sculptor and engraver, at the instigation of David's son, Adam. He is the well-known theatre and interior designer, and founder and artistic director of Musica nel Chiostro, Tuscany's annual opera festival in the restored, 17th-century Santa Croce monastery at Batignano. The company frequently stages first performances in modern times of forgotten early operas. It is also well-known in the operatic profession as a useful springboard, having launched many now famous directors, designers, conductors and singers on their careers. The festival's 'finest hour', according to *The Times*,[20] was engaging Italo Calvino to write a script for Mozart's unfinished singspiel *Zaide*. This has since been performed far and wide. In the spring of 1995, Adam put on a fundraising gala performance in London of a neglected work by Irving Berlin, *Watch Your Step*. Adam found the score in a second-hand bookshop in London.

64 Wiggonholt church, where David Pollock was churchwarden and is buried.

Conclusion

So now I am coming to the end of my story. I have tried to set down as honestly as I can the results of my inquiries. No doubt there are faults and flaws of fact and date in this account. Some mysteries still remain unresolved. Future generations may discover the answers to these questions, as more and more documents become available. At the time of writing, several mysteries remain: was Humphrey Baskerville the mercer really the son of Sir James Baskerville of Erdisley? On this hang some of our links to medieval times. Who was Agnes Bohun? Was John Curtis or his wife Elizabeth of Irish descent? Were the Dangars really Huguenots? Most mystifying of all, what became of Joseph Bennett?

I think I can safely say that I have traced our family back through its different branches, male and female, to the early history of this island and revealed quite a number of interesting characters along the way. We should be proud to be the products of all these hundreds of ancestors, successful or humble, well-off or struggling, famous or obscure, all of whom have contributed to our genes. Let us hope we can find within ourselves the hardiness of the Scots, the compassion and humour of the Bennetts, the enterprise of the Dangars and the business acumen of Ambrose Crowley. The people who started without advantages and made their own way are perhaps especially to be admired. We can honour all their memories by making the best of our own lives and leaving something worthwhile behind for future generations.

SUSAN CURTIS-BENNETT

Notes

[1] E.C. Rowland, 'The Life and Times of Henry Dangar', *Journal and Proceedings of Royal Australian Historical Society* (D.S. Ford, Sydney, 1953), p.5.

[2] B. Burke, *History of the Colonial Gentry* (Harrison & Sons, 1891), vol.1, pp.21-2.

[3] E.M. Dangar, *The Dangars from St Neot* (privately printed, 1964).

[4] S. Stephens, 'The Trial of the Huguenots', *Family History Monthly* (February, 1996), pp.28-33.

[5] 1915-18, vol.11, p.274.

[6] Rowland, *op.cit.*, p.6.

[7] *Rouse Hill House and the Rouses*, Western Australia (1988), *passim*.

[8] *Australian Dictionary of Biography, 1851-1890* (Melbourne University Press, 1972), pp.14-15.

[9] Roll of Graduates, University of Aberdeen, 1860-1900, W. Johnston, p.330.

[10] *Scottish Notes and Queries*, 3rd series, vol.1, p.81.

[11] A. and H. Taylor, *The House of Forbes* (Aberdeen University Press, 1937), pedigree no.26.

[12] *The Times*, 3 September 1996.

[13] 22 June 1996.

[14] 13 December 1918.

[15] *Roll of Graduates, University of Aberdeen 1860-1900* (Aberdeen University Press), p.330.

[16] *Roll of Graduates, University of Aberdeen 1901-1925* (Aberdeen University Press), p.357.

[17] M.D. Allardyce (ed.), *Roll of Service in the Great War 1914-1919* (Aberdeen University Press, 1921), p.279.

[18] John Pollock, *Times's Chariot* (John Murray, 1950).

[19] J. Slim, *Freshfields* (1993).

[20] 23 February 1995.

APPENDIX

SIGNATURES OF EIGHT GENERATIONS

[signature]   The Revd. Samuel Bennett BD

[signature]   The Revd. Dr. Samuel Bennett DD

[signature]   The Revd. George Peter Bennett BD

[signature]   Sir Henry Curtis Bennett Kt JP

[signature]   Emily, Lady Curtis-Bennett

[signature]   Sir Henry Honywood Curtis-Bennett Kt KC

[signature]   Violet Muriel Curtis-Bennett

[signature]   Frederick Henry [Derek] Curtis-Bennett QC

[signature]   Elsie Ann Curtis-Bennett (later Goode)

[signature]   David Dangar Henry Honywood Curtis-Bennett

[signature]   Mark Henry Tatlock Curtis-Bennett

SOURCES FOR FAMILY HISTORY RESEARCH

IN LONDON:
Bank of England Archive
British Library
Charity Commissioners
Church of England Record Office
College of Arms
Corporation of London Records Office
Dr Williams' s Library
Family Records Centre
Foreign and Commonwealth Office
Guildhall Library
The Huguenot Society and Library
Institute of Historical Research, University of London
International Genealogical Index
Lambeth Palace Library
The Law Society
Lincoln's Inn
London Metropolitan Archives
Manorial Society
Marylebone Cricket Club, Lord's Ground
The Mercers' Company of London
Merchant Taylors' School
Ministry of Defence
National Maritime Museum
National Register of Archives
Oriental and India Office Library and Records
Public Record Office
Royal College of Surgeons of England
The Royal Commission on Historical Documents
Royal Commission on the Historical Monuments of England
Salters' Company
Society of Antiquaries
Society of Genealogists
Somerset House
Wellcome Institute for the History of Medicine
Westminster Abbey Muniment Room and Library
Westminster Central Reference Library
Westminster City Archives
Westminster School
Wimbledon Lawn Tennis Museum
Worshipful Company of Goldsmiths

IN THE REGIONS:
Ashford Independent School for Girls, Kent
Belmont Abbey, Hereford
Blount/Blunt One Name Society, Kidderminster
Bodleian Library, Oxford
Borthwick Institute of Historical Research, York
Bristol Record Office
Buckinghamshire Record Office, Aylesbury
Cambridge University Archives
Canterbury Cathedral, City and Diocesan Record Office
Central Library, Aberdeen
Centre for Kentish Studies, Maidstone
Country Houses Association, Aynho, Oxon.
Dorking Museum, West Street
Durham Record Office
Essex Record Office, Chelmsford and Colchester
Essex Society for Family History
Federation of Family History Societies, Birmingham
General Register for Scotland, Edinburgh
Gloucester Cathedral diocesan library
Gloucestershire Record Office
Guildford Local Studies Library
Hampshire Record Office, Winchester
Herefordshire Record Office
Institute of Heraldic and Genealogical Studies, Canterbury
Local Studies Department, Shropshire Libraries, Shrewsbury
Marischal College Library, Aberdeen
National Library of Scotland, Edinburgh
North East Scotland Library Services, Old Meldrum
Norton Bavant Manor, Wiltshire
Peterhouse, Emmanuel, Jesus and Magdalene Colleges, Cambridge
Public Library, Dorking
Pythouse, Tisbury, Wiltshire
Queen Mother Library, King's College, Aberdeen
Rochester upon Medway Studies Centre
Royal Archives, Windsor
Salisbury Journal, Wiltshire
Shropshire Record Office, Shrewsbury
Surrey Record Office, Kingston-upon-Thames
West Surrey Family History Society
Wiltshire Archaeological Society, Devizes
Wiltshire Record Office, Trowbridge
Worcester Record Office

OVERSEAS:
Cathedral of the Holy Trinity, Gibraltar
Chamber of Mines of South Africa, Johannesburg
Channel Islands Family History Society
Department of Archives and History, Atlanta, Georgia, USA
The Genealogical Society of Victoria, Melbourne
Registry of Births, Death and Marriages, Gibraltar
Société de l'Histoire du Protestantisme Français, Paris

ADDITIONAL BIBLIOGRAPHY

Addison, W., *Essex Worthies* (Phillimore, Chichester, 1973)

Ainsworth, W.H., *The Flitch of Bacon* (Routledge, 1854)

Angus-Butterworth, M., *Old Cheshire Families and their seats* (E.J. Morton, Manchester, 1970)

The Australian Encyclopaedia (Melbourne University Press, 1966)

Baldwin, D., *Chapel Royal ancient and modern* (Duckworth, 1990)

Banks, T.C., *Baronies in Fee* (Harrison, Ripon, 1844), vol.1

Bebbington, G., *London Street Names* (Batsford, 1972)

Bennett, J., *A Memoir of the Bennett Family of South Wilts* (privately printed, Alderbury, 1958)

Bourne, S. and Chicken, A., *Records of the Church of England* (Prospect Litho, Maidstone, 1988)

Boyd, P., *Marriage Index, London Burials* and *Citizens of London*

Camp, A., *Wills and their Whereabouts* (pub. by the author, 1974)

Charnock, J., *Biographia Navalis* (R. Faulder, 1794)

Coldham, P.W., *American Loyalist Claims* (National Genealogical Society, Washington DC, 1980), vol.1

Crockford's *Clerical Directory*

Crowley, A., *Frauds in Nails detected* (London *c.*1700) (Guildhall Library)

Debrett's *Baronetage, Knightage and Companionage*

Dobson, D., *Directory of Scottish Settlers 1625-1825* (Genealogical Publishing Co., Baltimore, 1986), vol.2

The Essex Review

Field, J., *The King's Nurseries – the Story of Westminster School* (James & James, 1987)

Foss, E., *1066-187 Judges of England* (John Murray, 1870)

Gentleman's Magazine series

Gilbert, Martin, *Sir Horace Rumbold – portrait of a diplomat 1869-1941* (Heinemann, 1973)

Hackman, H., *Wates' Book of London Churchyards* (Collins, 1981)

Hanwell, W., *Pythouse and the Benetts* (Country Houses Association, 1984)

Hasted, E., *History and Topography of the County of Kent* (E.P. Publishing, reprinted 1972), vol.12

Hasted, E., *History of Canterbury* (Simmons & Kirby, Canterbury, 1808)

Haygarth, *MCC Scores and Biographies* (Frederick Lillywhite, 1862), vol.1

Heal, A., *The London Goldsmiths, 1200-1800* (Cambridge University Press, 1935)

Holmes, B., *The London Burial Grounds* (Macmillan, New York, 1896)

Jackson, Sir Richard, *Occupied with Crime* (George Harrap, 1967)

Kelway, A.C., *Memorials of Old Essex* (Bemrose, 1908)

Kingdom, G., *A Guide to Pythouse and the Ben(n)etts of Pythouse* (Country Houses Association, 5th edn, 1968)

London Topographical Record, ed. A. Saunders (1980), vol.24

Mackenzie, M., *Shoulder to Shoulder* (Penguin Books, Middlesex, 1975)

Marshall, J., *Royal Naval Biography* (Longman, Hurst, Rees, Orme & Brown, 1827)

Milne, A.G., *Eltham in Past Time* (Blackheath Press, 1910)

Morris, J., 'The Provosts and Bailiffs of Shrewsbury', *Transactions of the Shropshire Archaeological Society*, 3rd series

Neale, J.P., *History and Antiquities of the Abbey Church of St Peter, Westminster* (printed for Hurst, Robinson, 1823), vol.2

Orridge, B.B., *Citizens of London 1060-1867* (William Tegg, 1867)

Owen and Blakeway, *History of Shrewsbury* (Harding, Lepard & Co, 1825), vol.1

Robertson, M. (ed.), *The Encyclopaedia of Tennis* (Allen and Unwin, 1974)

Shaw, W.A., *Knights of England* (Sherratt & Hughes, 1906)

Sims, R., *Index to Pedigrees and Arms contained in Heralds' Visitations and other Genealogical Manuscripts at the British Museum* (1840)

Smith, D.B., *Commissioned Sea Officers of the Royal Navy, 1660-1815*

Steer, F., *History of the Dunmow Flitch Ceremony* (Essex Record Office, 1951)

Transactions of the Monumental Brass Society, 1969-1974 (Headley Bros, 1976), vol.11

Watson, I., *Westminster and Pimlico Past* (Historical Publications, 1993)

Weinreb, B. and Hibbert, C., *London Encyclopaedia* (Macmillan, 1983)

White, H.L., *Monuments and their Inscriptions* (Society of Genealogists, 1987)

Woodhead, J.R., *The Rulers of London 1660-1689* (London & Middlesex Archaeological Society, 1965)

Yorke, Philip, *The Royal Tribes of Wales* (I. Foulkes, Liverpool, 1887)

Young, G., *Poor Fred, the People's Prince* (Oxford University Press, 1937)

Young, W.A., *The Story of Sir Ambrose Crowley and his son John Crowley, 1659-1728* (Newcomen Society, 1923-24), vol.4 (Guildhall Library)

INDEX

Note: references to illustrations are in **bold type**; women are generally indexed under their own family names, where known; references to people featured in pedigree charts are in *italics*. The following abbreviations have been used: h. = husband; w. = wife; fa. = father; moth. = mother; s. = son; dau. = daughter; gr-gr. fa. = great-grandfather; b. = born; d. = died.

NOTES